Stanley Green

THE BROADWAY MUSICAL

A Picture Quiz Book

Dover Publications, Inc.

New York

Preface & Acknowledgments

This book contains 230 photographs of scenes from Broadway and off-Broadway musicals from 1903 to the end of 1975. The photographs are arranged in sections devoted to such categories as composers, performers, long runs, etc. Each question or answer contains the complete title of a musical, the year of its opening, its composer and lyricist, the names of all the featured performers in the scenes (except for an unidentifiable few) and other pertinent information. At times unavoidable overlapping of categories will cause a player or a production to appear in an unexpected section of the book. The index, therefore, is of help in locating pictures of performers or shows of particular interest.

Thanks are due the Theatre Collection, The New York Public Library at Lincoln Center, Astor, Lenox and Tilden Foundations, for permission to reproduce the following copyrighted photographs: 5, 9, 10, 12, 14, 22, 25, 26, 27, 28, 29, 32, 34, 35, 36, 45, 53, 54, 57, 60, 61, 62, 65, 66, 70, 72, 73, 98, 117, 118, 119, 120, 123, 124, 125, 128, 131, 136, 137, 138, 152, 162, 166, 180, 186, 193, 197, 200, 206.

I also appreciate the cooperation of the following people: Paul Myers, Dorothy Swerdlove and the staff of the Theatre Collection; Thomas Diffley of the Lynn Farnol Group, Inc.; Lee Snider of Chappell Music, Inc.; Louis Botto; Edward Jablonski; Hilda Schneider of the Irving Berlin Music Corp.; Hisako Hayami of the Toho Co., Ltd., Tokyo; and Louis Rachow of the Walter Hampden Library at The Players.

S. G.

Other Books by Stanley Green

The World of Musical Comedy
The Rodgers and Hammerstein Story
The ASCAP Biographical Dictionary (editor)
Ring Bells! Sing Songs!
Starring Fred Astaire
Encyclopaedia of the Musical Theatre

Published in Canada by General Publishing Company, Ltd., 30 Lesmill Road, Don Mills, Toronto, Ontario.
Published in the United Kingdom by Constable and Company, Ltd., 10 Orange Street, London WC 2.

The Broadway Musical: A Picture Quiz Book is a new work, first published by Dover Publications, Inc., in 1977.

International Standard Book Number: 0-486-23403-7

Manufactured in the United States of America
Dover Publications, Inc.
180 Varick Street
New York, N.Y. 10014

Contents

Operettas

1–6

Lush, melodious operetta may have had its roots in Vienna but thanks to Victor Herbert, Sigmund Romberg and Rudolf Friml, it easily thrived on Broadway during the early decades of this century.

1. A successor to *The Wizard of Oz*, this operetta was all about a boy and girl who take a trip to the land of Mother Goose. They are seen here singing "I Can't Do the Sum," accompanied by a chorus tapping chalk on slates. What was the name of the musical and who composed the score?

2. Victor Herbert wrote *Mlle. Modiste* (1905) for a tiny, slim-waisted prima donna who had previously sung at the Metropolitan. Who was she, and what was the imploring ballad in this operetta with which her name was always associated?

3. Soldiers in operettas were always elegantly caparisoned—as they so obviously were in the 1910 success *The Spring Maid*. Can you identify the star? (She sang "Day Dreams, Visions of Bliss.")

4. Peering from behind the roses are Howard Marsh and Ilse Marvenga, as crown prince and waitress, in what tender operetta extolling the golden days of youth? Also name the composer and at least 2 of the most famous numbers sung by the prince.

5. A vigorous call to arms set pulses pounding during this scene from a 1925 Rudolf Friml operetta about French poet François Villon. What was the name of the production, the name of the rabble-rousing song being sung and the name of the singer seen here as Villon?

6. Johann Strauss's *Die Fledermaus* was mounted on Broadway in 4 different English-language versions. Seen here are Helen Ford and Kitty Carlisle (in her Broadway debut as Prince Orlovsky) in the version titled (a) *The Merry Countess*, 1912; (b) *A Wonderful Night*, 1929; (c) *Champagne, Sec*, 1933; (d) *Rosalinda*, 1942.

George M. Cohan

7–10

Broadway's Yankee Doodle Boy (1878–1942) wrote, directed and—for the most part—starred in 21 musical comedies (including 2 for which he contributed half the songs) between 1901 and 1928.

---

7. The final scene from a Cohan success of 1906 shows heroine Mary Jane Jenkins tearing up the will that would make her wealthy so that her proud boyfriend, Kid Burns, will give his consent to wed her. Who played the parts, what was the name of the show, and what were its 3 most enduring songs?

8. The superpatriotic hero of *George Washington, Jr.* (1906) adopted the name of the father of his country, wrapped himself in Old Glory and sang a song to show his affection for the flag. What was the song? In this scene, Cohan, in the title role, looks none too willing to accept the hand of his Anglophilic father, a United States senator. Who played the father?

George M. Cohan

continued

9. Cohan seems a bit pop-eyed at the antics of Polly Walker, with whom he appeared in what 1927 musical?

10. The only time Cohan acted in a musical he did not write himself was when he portrayed Franklin D. Roosevelt, the only American President ever to be the main character in a Broadway song-and-dance show. The name of the musical was (a) *Hold Your Hats, Boys;* (b) *Mr. President;* (c) *1600 Pennsylvania Avenue;* (d) *I'd Rather Be Right;* (e) none of the above. Who wrote the score and the libretto?

Irving Berlin

11–16

Between 1914 and 1962, the music and lyrics of Irving Berlin (born 1888) reflected the spirit of his country in his scores for 19 Broadway shows (including 2 for which he wrote half the songs).

---

11. Berlin's first, and predominantly ragtime, Broadway score was written in 1914 for a revue-type musical that spot-lighted the most celebrated ballroom dancers of their day. What was the show and who were the dancers? What was the memorable contrapuntal song from the score?

12. From 1921 to 1924, Berlin created the scores for a series of 4 annual *Music Box Revues* that were celebrated for their scenic beauty, innovations in stagecraft and melodic distinction. During the run of the 1924 edition, a song was added and sung by the 2 artists pictured here. What was it? Who are they?

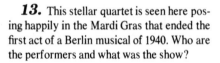

13. This stellar quartet is seen here posing happily in the Mardi Gras that ended the first act of a Berlin musical of 1940. Who are the performers and what was the show?

14. Irving Berlin's all-soldier show *This Is the Army* (1942) opened with the stage crowded with khaki-clad minstrels. Can you identify at least one of the soldiers in the foreground and the name of the song they are singing?

15. *Annie Get Your Gun* (1946) was a bull's-eye hit for both composer-lyricist Berlin and star Ethel Merman. What is the name of the song that was used to convince sharpshooting hillbilly Annie Oakley that she should join Buffalo Bill's Wild West Show? Who are the singers doing the convincing? Do you remember the names of the show's producers (they're better known as a composer and lyricist-librettist)? For extra credit, name the composer who was supposed to write the score but who died before production began.

16. Berlin's last Broadway musical was in 1962 and concerned the final days in office of a fictitious American President. What was the name of the show and who played the President and his lady (here shown back home after he has left office)?

Jerome Kern

17–23

Recognized as the father of the modern American musical, Jerome Kern (1885–1945) composed 34 Broadway scores (including 2 for which he wrote half the songs), mostly in collaboration with lyricists P. G. Wodehouse, Anne Caldwell, Oscar Hammerstein II and Otto Harbach. Kern's first show was in 1912 and his last in 1939.

———

17. Between 1915 and 1918, Kern wrote the music for a series of intimate musical comedies presented at the tiny Princess Theatre. Pictured here are the leads in the last one he wrote, *Oh, Lady! Lady!!* Can you identify them? What song was cut from the score before the opening but then became a show-stopper in *Show Boat*? Name at least two other Princess Theatre musicals.

18 & 19. Two scenes in *Show Boat* (1927), Kern's crowning achievement. At the end of Act I *(19)*, Parthy Ann Hawks unsuccessfully tries to get Gaylord Ravenal arrested for murder, while Parthy's husband, Cap'n Andy, gives his approval for Ravenal to marry their daughter Magnolia. Who played these parts in the original production? In Act II *(18)*, the vocalist perched on the piano is about to sing a somewhat revised version of the discarded song from *Oh, Lady! Lady!!* Who is she?

Jerome Kern
continued

20 & 21. A Jerome Kern/Otto Harbach musical of 1933 was set in Paris and dealt with the operations of a celebrated couturière's establishment. Can you identify the show and all of the actors shown in these 2 scenes? What happened to the actor leaning on the piano *(20)* after he quit acting?

22. Pictured here are 3 principals from a Jerome Kern/Oscar Hammerstein musical that was set in Edendorf (Bavaria) and Munich. Who are the actors and what was the musical? What was the name of the vaudeville partner of the man leaning out of the window, and what was their most celebrated song?

23. Ah, the eternal quadrangle! Do you know the names of at least 2 actors shown in this scene of romantic embarrassment that occurred in Kern's last Broadway musical, *Very Warm for May* (1939)? What enduring song was first heard in this show? Who was Kern's lyric-writing collaborator?

George & Ira Gershwin

24–27

Composer George Gershwin (1898–1937) and his brother, lyricist Ira Gershwin (born 1896), brought fresh vigor to the Broadway musical scene from their first collaboration in 1924 to their last in 1935. In addition to the 14 scores they wrote together (including one shared with another team), George wrote 9 with other lyricists and Ira wrote 6 with other composers.

24. The brothers collaborated on the songs for the first book musical to star the popular British actress on the right, who has just frightened everyone in this scene by popping a champagne cork. What was the show and who was the actress? Can you also identify the actor in the striped blazer and the actor holding the 2 plates? Name at least 2 of the 4 major songs from the score.

25. In 1929, the Gershwins (plus lyricist Gus Kahn) were involved with a Ziegfeld production, *Show Girl*, that featured a demure ingenue and the trio of raucous comedians surrounding her. Who is the girl and who are the boys? What song did the actress dance to in the show that prompted her new husband, during the Boston tryout, to rise from his orchestra seat and impulsively sing right along with the music?

26. What was the name of a Gershwin musical of 1930, set in Custerville, Arizona, that featured a young performer who would quickly win lasting stardom? In this scene she has just had a temporary estrangement from her boyfriend. Who is she, what song did she sing to express her unhappiness, and who is the sympathetic comedian on the right who also sang the song?

27. The Gershwin "folk-opera" *Porgy and Bess* was a financial flop in 1935, but a success in 1942. In both Broadway productions, the title roles were played by the same actors, shown here in a scene with J. Rosamond Johnson. Who are they? Who was the Bess in the 1953 touring revival that played Broadway?

Cole Porter

28–33

The urbane music and lyrics of Cole Porter (1891–1964) attracted theatregoers to 24 Broadway shows between 1916 and 1955.

---

28. Paris was the setting—but not the title—of what 1929 Cole Porter musical? Who is the straw-hatted American "Official Guide" seen here at the American Express office, and who is the rather dubious-looking lady? Can you name the 2 major songs from the score?

29. In order to get away from affairs of state, the royal couple in this musical pose as "Mr. and Mrs. Smith" and enjoy themselves at a public beach. Who played the parts? What was the musical? What song was sung in this scene? Name the 2 numbers that have become standards.

30. Who is the befuddled man (in the middle of the group) shown here on his way to what diplomatic post in what Cole Porter musical? Who played his wife, seen here to the right?

31. Though Ethel Merman and Bert Lahr were the acclaimed stars in this 1939 Broadway musical, these 2 performers were also well received and went on to achieve fame in the movies. What was the musical? Who are the performers, seen here doing the nightclub number "Ev'ry Day's a Holiday"?

Cole Porter

continued

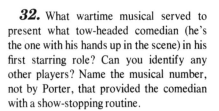

32. What wartime musical served to present what tow-headed comedian (he's the one with his hands up in the scene) in his first starring role? Can you identify any other players? Name the musical number, not by Porter, that provided the comedian with a show-stopping routine.

33. Who starred in Porter's last musical, *Silk Stockings*? Who starred in the movie on which the musical was based, and what was it called? Who starred in the film version of the musical?

Richard Rodgers
& Lorenz Hart

34–39

Richard Rodgers (born 1902) and Lorenz Hart (1895–1943) created highly adventuresome scores between 1920 and 1942 for 26 musicals (including one score shared with another team and one revived score augmented with new songs).

———

34. In 1925, Rodgers and Hart supplied the songs for a musical based on an incident in the American Revolution. In the first scene, the patriotic heroine was modestly clad in a barrel and armed with an umbrella to ward off the possible advances of a British officer who has just seen her swimming in the nude. What was the name of the show, who are these 2 actors, and what 3 love songs did they sing later in the production?

35. Rodgers and Hart's biggest hit in the 20s was based on a novel satirizing modern American technology when adopted by a legendary British kingdom. Who wrote the novel? What was the title of the show? Who played the title role, seen here being threatened by an armored knight? What 2 songs did he sing to woo his fair lady?

36. A 1928 Rodgers and Hart musical, *Present Arms*, dealt with the activities of Marines in and around Pearl Harbor. Can you identify these 3 performers—or at least the one on the left? What song did he introduce in the show?

37. Rodgers and Hart's landmark musical of 1936 took a satirical look at classical ballet. What was its name? In this scene, can you identify the company's patroness, its bearded impresario and its timid new choreographer-dancer? What was the show's leading romantic duet?

38. In this musical, the crash landing of a French pilot helps a Long Island community get funds to build an airfield. Pictured at the crash are a former movie child actress, the future lead in *Oklahoma!* and the future "Merry Mailman" of television. Who are they? What's the musical? How many of the Rodgers and Hart songs can you remember?

39. A fantasy about a Hungarian banker who marries a real angel was the theme of Rodgers and Hart's 1938 success *I Married an Angel.* Who played the angel and who played the banker, pictured here on their wedding night? What song is being sung? Who else was starred in the show?

Richard Rodgers & Oscar Hammerstein II

40–43

Between 1943 and 1960, Rodgers and Oscar Hammerstein II (1895–1960) created the music and lyrics for 9 Broadway productions that established them as the most influential writers of the postwar period.

———

40. The comic lovers of the team's first musical, *Oklahoma!* (1943), were named Ado Annie Carnes and Will Parker. Who played the roles? What was the name of Ado Annie's self-describing solo, and the name of her duet with Will in which they explained their romantic preferences? From what play was the musical adapted?

41. In 1953, Rodgers and Hammerstein wrote a backstage musical whose main romance concerned an assistant stage manager and an understudy. Name the show. Who played the roles, and what is the duet they are singing in this scene? What song in the show was first called "Beneath the Southern Cross" when it was part of the score for the television documentary *Victory at Sea*?

42. The final scene from a 1958 musical in which a Chinese picture bride, recently arrived in San Francisco, explains to the assembled wedding guests why she cannot marry the man to whom she has been contracted. What was the play? What was the explanation? Who played the recalcitrant bride? Who is the actor in the light silk jacket?

43. "Be wise, compromise," is the advice the 2 on the right give to the man with the guitar, but he remains firm in his opposition to the Nazi takeover of his country. Who played these roles in the Rodgers and Hammerstein *Sound of Music* (1959), and what song are they singing?

Leading Ladies

44–51

44. The actress on the right, then only 18, was still in music school when she took over the leading female role in *The Blue Paradise* (1915), just 4 days before the Broadway opening. Who is the actress, seen here with Ted Lorraine and Teddy Webb (he is apparently choking on a loaf of bread)? Who composed the operetta and what song did the actress introduce?

45. The last Broadway appearance of this gingham-clad actress was in a successful nautical musical with a score by Vincent Youmans, Leo Robin and Clifford Grey. Name the actress and her show. Name her co-star. Name their most memorable duet. What previous hit with Youmans music did the actress also star in?

46. Who was the saucy French actress who introduced Cole Porter's "Let's Do It" in this production? What was the production? Whose dance band appeared on stage to accompany the star?

47. One of the theatre's great torch singers scored a great success in this scene from a 1929 revue. Who was she? What was the name of the revue? Who appeared with her in the scene? What was the song she sang in it?

Leading Ladies

continued

48. A film and television actress as well as Broadway leading lady, this actress is seen here in an unconventional musical about marriage by Kurt Weill and Alan Jay Lerner. Who is she and what was the name of the musical? Who was her co-star?

49. Though she has made relatively few appearances in the Broadway theatre, this Berlin-born actress-singer has become something of a legend. Here she is seen in an English-language version of what musical in which she had appeared in Berlin 26 years before? What was her famous solo and who wrote it?

50. Trying to make herself look old with the help of a mop, glasses and shawl, this character's true identity is apparently being discovered by the man she loves. Who played these parts and what was the musical in which they appeared? Can you name the most popular songs the actress introduced?

51. Who is the actress, playing a shipboard social director, shown here with her young charges in *Sail Away* (1961)? What is she singing and who wrote it?

Marilyn Miller

52–55

Broadway's twinkling dancing star Marilyn Miller (1898–1936) appeared in 12 productions between 1914 and 1933.

———

52. Miss Miller as she looked in *Sally* (1920), her first starring vehicle. What was the reason for the costume she is wearing here? Who were the 2 male comedians who appeared in the show? Who wrote the score? Name the most famous song.

53. Seen here are the principal players in Miss Miller's 1925 vehicle, which dealt with a bareback rider in an English circus who finds true love in America. What was the name of the show? Can you name at least 3 of the players besides Miss Miller? What were the leading songs in the Jerome Kern/Otto Harbach/Oscar Hammerstein score?

54. In the musical *Rosalie* (1928), Marilyn Miller had the services of what 2 major composers who divided the score-writing chore? What historical event was the "inspiration" for the musical?

55. Miss Miller's last Broadway appearance was in a revue created in the form of a newspaper. What was it called? Who wrote the songs? Who wrote the sketches? In this scene, depicting the influence of Noël Coward on the help at a New York hotel from which he has just departed, Miss Miller is shown with . . .?

Al Jolson

56 & 57

Appearing in 12 musicals between 1911 and 1950, Al Jolson (1886–1950) was the self-styled "World's Greatest Entertainer."

56. Seen here with a showgirl, Al appeared in what 1918 musical success that introduced characters from the *Arabian Nights*? What was the early George Gersh-win hit that Al interpolated in the show during its post-Broadway tour? Who was its lyricist?

57. In this 1925 musical, Al played a stableboy who ends up riding a horse to victory in the Kentucky Derby. What was the name of the horse? What was the name of the show? What song, later identified with Eddie Cantor, was introduced in this production?

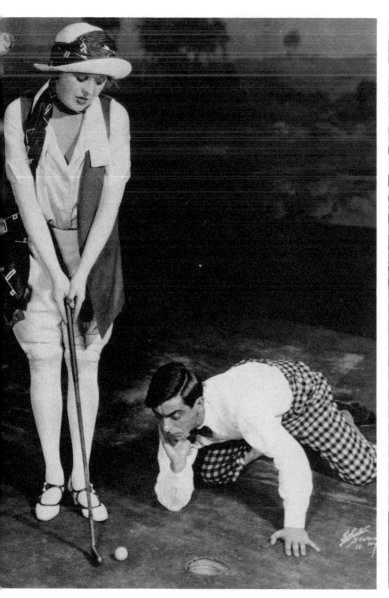

Eddie Cantor

58 & 59

Between 1917 and 1941, energetic, eye-popping Eddie Cantor (1892–1964) was seen in 10 Broadway productions.

58. Eddie played a caddy master in this musical billed as "A Musical Comedy of Palm Beach and Golf." What was it called? Can you recognize the golfer trying

not to be unnerved by Cantor's stare?

59. The comedian's last Broadway stage appearance in 1941 found him again concerned with a popular sport. What was the sport and the name of the show? Does the girl on the far right of the picture look familiar? What was the play from which this musical was adapted? Can you name another musical that came along 20 years later that was also based on the same play?

Gertrude Lawrence

60–63

The gossamer grace of Gertrude Lawrence (1898–1952) was a feature of 8 Broadway musicals produced between 1924 and 1952.

60. Miss Lawrence as she appeared in a 1930 show, Lew Leslie's *International Revue*. Who was her ebullient co-star and what was their main duet? What German-accented teller of tall stories was also in the cast?

61. In 1936, Miss Lawrence co-starred with Noël Coward in a program of 9 one-act plays, which Coward also wrote. Name the overall title of the program and also the 3 one-act musicals that were included in the production.

62. A musical dealing with the unlikely subject of psychoanalysis came to Broadway in 1941. What was it called? Who is the virile circus performer seen with Miss Lawrence in a dream sequence? What was Miss Lawrence's show-stopping number in this sequence and who wrote it?

63. Gertrude Lawrence's final stage appearance was in what musical set in the Far East? What song did she and young Sandy Kennedy (as her son) sing in this first scene in the play? Can you name at least one of the actresses who took over the part after Miss Lawrence's death?

Beatrice Lillie

64–67

The antics of Canadian-born Beatrice Lillie (born 1894) delighted Broadway audiences in 13 musicals from 1924 to 1964.

---

64. In 1928, Beatrice Lillie drank a toast with what future film star in the musical *She's My Baby*? Can you name the composer and lyricist of the show, and also the ingenue, who had a far greater success in Hollywood than on Broadway?

65. The same year, Miss Lillie also co-starred on Broadway in a revue written by Noël Coward. What was it called and who was her co-star? (In this pantomime sketch dealing with the hazards of queuing up for a bus, Miss Lillie is seen third from the right.)

66. A sketch about a Russian spy was one of the comic highlights of a 1939 Noël Coward revue in which Miss Lillie starred. Name the revue. Do you recognize the actor playing the officer enamored by the glamorous secret agent (he was known for his fish mimicry)? Name at least 2 musical numbers that involved Miss Lillie.

67. In this scene from *High Spirits* (1964), Miss Lillie's last Broadway musical, she appeared as a spiritualist trying to exorcise a rather troublesome ghost. Who is the concerned gentleman at the left and who is the ghost? From what play was the musical adapted?

Fred Astaire

68–71

Fred Astaire (born 1899), the stage's most gifted dancing star, appeared in 11 Broadway musicals between 1917 and 1932, all but the last with his sister Adele.

68. Fred and Adele Astaire won major Broadway recognition in 1922. What was the name of the show in which they scored their first big success? For extra credit, can you remember the name given the simple step that became the dancers' trademark? For more extra credit, what was the musical called when it was presented in London?

69. Here's Fred surrounded by the ostrich-plumed lovelies of the chorus of *Lady, Be Good!* (1924). Can you name 2 of the 3 numbers that Fred and Adele introduced together in the show? Who wrote the words and music? What famous song, though written for this musical, was dropped during the tryout?

70. In this Gershwin musical of 1927, Fred performed one of his rare dance routines with a partner other than his sister. What was the musical? Who was the girl? What is the number being performed in this scene?

71. Fred's only stage appearance without his sister found him dancing with what partner in what musical? Name the show's hit song and its composer. Do you recognize the actor in the dressing gown? What was the name of the film version of the musical?

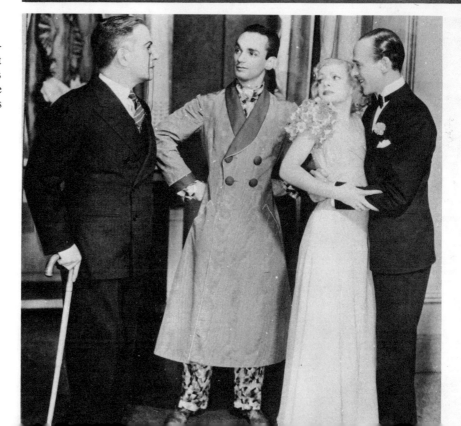

Ethel Merman

72–78

Since beginning her Broadway career in 1930, Ethel Merman (born 1909) has won acclaim in 14 musicals.

———

72. Miss Merman's first Broadway appearance was in what 1930 show? What was this show-stopping number at a dude ranch? What was her other big song in the production?

73. A 1934 musical taking place aboard an ocean liner gave Ethel Merman—as Reno Sweeney—a chance to outtrumpet Gabriel in a scene at a ship's party. What was the show, the song and the composer? Who were Ethel's co-stars?

74. Ethel Merman's 1936 musical *Red, Hot and Blue!* found her involved with the gentleman in the striped polo outfit. Who is he and why the odd getup? Who was the third star in the show? What were the most popular Cole Porter songs that Ethel sang in it?

75. In a dream sequence from *DuBarry Was a Lady* (1939), Ethel appeared as Du-Barry and Bert Lahr as Louis XV. What was the reason for the dream and who did the dreaming? Do you know the name of the star originally sought for the role Miss Merman played?

Ethel Merman

continued

76. Backed by local Canal Zone lads and lassies (including, at the extreme right, June Allyson), Panama Hattie is all dolled up as she awaits the arrival of her divorced fiancé's 8-year-old daughter. Ethel, of course, played Hattie in this 1940 smash, but do you recall the name of the girl who played Hattie's future stepdaughter? Or the Cole Porter song they introduced together? What energetic blonde introduced "Fresh as a Daisy"?

77. This role found Ethel Merman playing a thinly disguised real-life female ambassador to a small European country. What was the show and who was Miss Merman's leading man, here making his only appearance in a musical? Name the real Washington party-giver turned ambassador who "inspired" the show.

78. Ethel Merman's favorite Broadway role was in what 1959 musical based on the memoirs of what famous public undresser? Name the song being sung in this scene and the other people in the picture. Name at least 2 other songs introduced by Ethel, and the collaborators on the score.

Mary Martin

79–84

Mary Martin (born 1913), from Weatherford, Texas, first charmed New York in 1938 and has since had leading roles in 8 Broadway musicals.

———

79. In her Broadway debut, Mary Martin played a naïve but accommodating young lady who somehow got stranded in Siberia and somehow felt the urge to shed her clothing. Name the musical, the song she sang and the man who wrote it. And who could that parka-clad hoofer be standing to Miss Martin's immediate left?

80. As Venus in her first starring role on Broadway, Miss Martin is shown here helping herself to a lady's suit displayed in a couturier's window. What was the name of the musical? Who is the gentleman offering his hand to the goddess? What was the song Miss Martin sang shortly after this encounter? Who wrote the score for the musical?

81. Though she never played this role on Broadway, Miss Martin toured in it and did it on television. What was the part and what was the show? Who did play the part on Broadway?

82. In Rodgers and Hammerstein's *South Pacific* (1949), Ensign Nellie Forbush (Mary Martin) temporarily embarrasses Luther Billis by complimenting him on the care with which he has done her laundry. Who played Luther Billis? What comic song of frustration, sung by the sailors and Seabees, did this interlude interrupt?

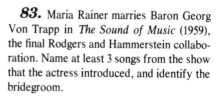

83. Maria Rainer marries Baron Georg Von Trapp in *The Sound of Music* (1959), the final Rodgers and Hammerstein collaboration. Name at least 3 songs from the show that the actress introduced, and identify the bridegroom.

84. In a post-wedding scene from Miss Martin's last Broadway musical, the actress exchanges glances with her co-star while seated on their fourposter bed. Who is he and what was the musical? What was the most memorable song in the score? What was the most unusual feature of the production?

Gwen Verdon

85–88

Broadway's leading dancing star for over 20 years has been Gwen Verdon (born 1926), who has appeared in 7 musicals to date.

———

85. Miss Verdon first attracted widespread notice—with, among other things, a torrid Apache dance partnered by Ralph Beaumont—in what musical? Who was the composer? Who was the single-named French star of the musical? For extra credit, name the first Broadway musical in which Miss Verdon appeared.

86. Achieving stardom in a musical that combined baseball with the Faust legend, Miss Verdon played a temptress who, in this scene, tries to console the show's hero, played by Stephen Douglass. What was the musical? What song are they singing? Who wrote it? Name Miss Verdon's 2 other main songs in the production.

Gwen Verdon

continued

87. Accidentally finding herself in the hotel suite of a famous Italian movie star— and with his autographed picture and top hat to prove it—Gwen Verdon bursts out in song to express her good fortune. What was the show? What was the song? Who wrote it? What Italian film was the basis for the musical's plot?

88. In 1975, Miss Verdon appeared on Broadway in a musical version of a 1926 play about a famous murder trial. What was the name of the play and what was the name of the musical? Who was Miss Verdon's co-star and what is the number they are doing in this scene?

Hello, Dollies!

89–96

89–96. The following 12 actresses played the role of Dolly Gallagher Levi in *Hello, Dolly!*, both in New York and in major U.S. touring companies:

  (a) Eve Arden
  (b) Pearl Bailey
  (c) Thelma Carpenter
  (d) Carol Channing
  (e) Phyllis Diller
  (f) Betty Grable
  (g) Dorothy Lamour
  (h) Mary Martin
  (i) Ethel Merman
  (j) Bibi Osterwald
  (k) Martha Raye
  (l) Ginger Rogers

Match the names with the 8 photographs and indicate whether the actress played the role in New York or on the road. In all but one picture, the actresses are seen as they appeared at a turn-of-the-century night spot. Can you name it? Can you also name the show's Broadway producer and director-choreographer?

91

Hello, Dollies!
continued

93

94

Hello, Dollies!

continued

Black Stars

97–106

97. The first black star to win acclaim on Broadway, primarily in 8 *Ziegfeld Follies* between 1910 and 1919, was originally a member of a 2-man vaudeville team. Can you name the entertainer, seen here (at the right) with his partner, George W. Walker, in an all-black musical called *In Dahomey* (1903)? What was the song with which he was most closely identified?

98. The first long-run all-black musical opened in 1921 and dealt with a mayoralty election in Dixieland's Jimtown. What was the name of the show? Who played the leads, shown here as the victorious candidate and the defeated candidate who is now the police chief? Name the 2 song hits from the Eubie Blake/Noble Sissle score.

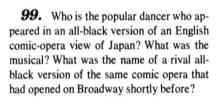

99. Who is the popular dancer who appeared in an all-black version of an English comic-opera view of Japan? What was the musical? What was the name of a rival all-black version of the same comic opera that had opened on Broadway shortly before?

100. An all-black fantasy that opened on Broadway in 1940 gave the actress pictured here her greatest role in a musical. Who is she? Who is the actor in the scene with her? What was the musical? The score for the production was created by (a) Vernon Duke and John Latouche; (b) Duke Ellington and Johnny Mercer; (c) Harold Arlen and E. Y. Harburg; (d) George and Ira Gershwin; (e) none of the above. Name Miss Waters' show-stopping song.

101. Opera came to Broadway in 1943 when a French work with a Spanish locale was updated and relocated to the American South during World War II. What was the title of the French opera and what was the title of the Broadway musical? Who was the composer and who did the adaptation? Name the actress strutting in the foreground of this scene and the aria she is singing.

102. Who is this exuberant entertainer shown here in what 1956 Broadway vehicle? Who are the men on either side of him? Name 2 popular songs that emerged from the score by Jerry Bock, Larry Holofcener and George Weiss.

Black Stars

continued

103. The song stylist on the right starred in a 1957 musical set in the Caribbean. Who is she and what was the show? Name the main songs she sang in the Harold Arlen/E. Y. Harburg score. Who is the Mexican-born actor with whom she costarred? For extra credit, name the production in which the singer made her first Broadway appearance (it wasn't in a musical).

104. At an elegant party in Paris, fashion model Barbara Woodruff angrily turns on David Jordan, who loves her, because he has criticized her relationship with a wealthy Parisian. Who played Barbara and what song is she singing? Who played David? What's the musical, and who wrote its songs?

105. The adventures of Charlemagne's son provided the basis for this successful 1972 musical, in which the actor peeking out from between the 2 girls was known as The First Player. Who is the actor, what is the musical, and what is the song he is singing to introduce the story? The show's director was (a) Bob Fosse; (b) Gower Champion; (c) Michael Bennett; (d) Harold Prince; (e) none of the above.

106. The gift of a heart was ecstatically received by what character in what successful 1974 musical? What was the name of the 1903 musical that was adapted from the same source, and what was that source?

Funny Girls

107–116

107. The rotund singer on the right isn't thought of today as a comedienne but that was the way she was cast in her 2 Broadway musicals. The first was *Honeymoon Lane* (1926); the second, in which she is pictured here, was *Flying High* (1930). Who is she? What song did she introduce in this show and who wrote it? Who is the grinning comic talking into the microphone?

108. This trio of comic stars appeared together in the 1931 revue *Crazy Quilt*. What are their names? To whom was the lady married at the time? What popular song did the threesome sing? What was the name of the original version of the revue, which played on Broadway in 1930, and who had the starring parts?

109. The queen of deadpan delivery is seen here in a sketch from the "newspaper" revue, *As Thousands Cheer* (1933). Who is she and whom is she impersonating? Who are the other people being impersonated?

110. Although this routine was performed in a revue called *New Faces* (1934), the elfin comedienne in the polo coat had made her Broadway debut as early as 1925. Who is she and what is she doing?

111. A scene from what musical based on what play by Eugene O'Neill? Who is the actress seen here with Gwen Verdon? Who wrote the score?

112. Name the diminutive slack-jawed comedienne caught here trying to lift her skirt, to the obvious embarrassment of Phil Silvers. What was the musical? Who are the men seated around the table? What was the comedienne's show-stopping number, and who wrote it?

113. Playing a hoydenish silver-mine owner, the actress shown here second from the left throws a party for her titled friends to impress Denver society. What is the actress' name and the name of the musical? Can you identify 2 of the other 5 principals in the scene? Who wrote the score, which included "I Ain't Down Yet"?

114. The Incomparable Rosalie and Marco the Magnificent engaged in one of their frequent spats during this sword act in what 1961 musical? Who was the exuberant comedienne, who was the graceful swordsman, and what Bob Merrill song did they sing in this scene? Do you also recall the name of the languid postmeridian ballad that the actress introduced in *The Golden Apple*?

Funny Girls

continued

115. The first American musical set in Israel was *Milk and Honey* (1961), with songs by Jerry Herman. It was in this show that the actress pictured on the right, long a favorite of the Yiddish theatre, made her Broadway debut. Who is she? Who are the other 2?

116. A musical about Bill Robinson and Shirley Temple? No, in the 1964 Hollywood spoof *Fade Out—Fade In*, these 2 are supposed to be out-of-work actors who are reduced to wearing sandwich signs advertising a dancing school and a "Kiddie Kareer School." Who played the parts? Who wrote the song "You Mustn't Be Discouraged," which they are singing here to buck up their spirits?

Funny Boys

117–134

117. Formerly teamed with Dave Montgomery, the acrobatic comedian on the left is seen here with his daughter in the 1923 musical *Stepping Stones*. What is his name and what is his daughter's name? For what song by what writers are they costumed?

118. Who is this nemesis of children and animals, seen here playing a cello of his own making? What was the show and what was the name of the character he played?

119. Though the comedian with the diamond-patterned sweater was also on hand, it was the prizefighter with the knee-guards who got most of the laughs in this 1928 DeSylva/Brown/Henderson musical. Who are they and what is the name of the show? Name the outstanding song.

120. *Heads Up!* (1929), which was concerned with rum-running during Prohibition, offered this tense scene involving a stalwart Coast Guard officer, a villainous bootlegger and a beloved actor as a comic cook. Who are they? What was the song of unrequited love that the Coast Guardsman sang?

121. Sounding the call to battle is this comedy team that appeared in a 1930 satire on war. Who are they? What was the show? Who wrote the score, and what were the main songs? What durable ballad was part of the score of the original version of this show, which opened out of town in 1927 but never reached New York?

122. Name this 1944 Cole Porter show. In it one member of the above team played a con-man who has fled to Mexico to escape the law but finds himself in the spotlight after mistakenly catching the bull's ear at the Plaza de Toros. Who was he? Who was the lady bullfighter who threw the ear?

123. The zany sibling quartet as they appeared in (a) *I'll Say She Is;* (b) *The Cocoanuts;* (c) *Animal Crackers.* What is happening in this scene? Who is the woman in the hat just to the right of the podium? Who was responsible for the songs?

124. A popular 1930 musical, *Fine and Dandy,* starred the comedian on the right, who was known for his broad, innocent grin, his Rube-Goldberg-type contraptions and his story about 5 Hawaiians. What's his name? Can you also recall the name of his stooge, seen on the left, who later opened a celebrated restaurant in Hollywood? Who wrote the songs for the show?

125. This 1930 Ziegfeld production starred the comedian known as The Perfect Fool. Who is he and what was the name of the musical, which was peopled by characters out of Mother Goose fables? What Rodgers and Hart torch song, added to the score just before the New York opening, helped establish the fame of singer Ruth Etting?

126. Usually playing the wide-eyed innocent, the fellow with the golf club is seen here in the 1941 Rodgers and Hart musical *Higher and Higher*. His name is (a) Ted Healy; (b) Jack Haley; (c) Jack Whiting; (d) Johnny Dooley; (e) none of the above. Who stole the show?

Funny Boys

continued

127. Seen in his role as Pierre Ginsberg, the French professor, this Yiddish-accented clown was a favorite in revues and book shows. In which production did he first introduce this character? What was the name of his straight-man partner, with whom he appeared in 17 revues?

128. What is the name of the elephant? What is the name of the energetic comic? What was the show they were both in? Who created the score and what were at least 2 of the 3 chief numbers? What was the most unusual feature of the show?

129. In the sketch "The Pride of the Claghornes," from *The Band Wagon* (1931), who played the unyielding Southern colonel? He is distraught because his daughter (a) has started wearing bloomers; (b) is pregnant; (c) is a virgin; (d) loves a Yankee; (e) none of the above. Who are the other actors in this picture and who wrote the sketch? What songs by what songwriters did 2 of these performers introduce together in the show?

130. Who is the male comedian in this sketch from the *Ziegfeld Follies* of 1936? What character is Fanny Brice playing (which she based on the bratty kid character originated by the comedienne in *136*)? Who produced this edition of the *Follies*?

131. What is the name of this nimble comedian whose first major role found him as an effeminate fashion photographer who couldn't help swooning at the sight of his favorite male movie star? What was the musical? Who was the star of the musical (on the right)? What tongue-twisting number by Kurt Weill and Ira Gershwin did the comedian perform? For extra credit, name the first Broadway musical in which he appeared.

132. Just as fast-talking con-man Harrison Floy is about to skip off with his ill-gotten gains, he is stopped during a party scene in *High Button Shoes* (1947). Who played Floy? Can you recognize the 3 people trying to keep him from running off? Who wrote the score for this show, which included "Papa, Won't You Dance with Me?" and "I Still Get Jealous"?

133. In this his second Broadway musical, the versatile comedian on the right was required to play 7 different parts, including the French World War I ace, Val du Val. Who is the comic and what is the show? Who is the girl? Who wrote the book on which the libretto was based and which other one of his books was also transformed into a Broadway musical?

134. Who is the rotund comic on the right who scored impressively in this musical farce based on characters and situations created by Roman playwright Titus Maccius Plautus? What was the musical called? Who else is in the picture? Name the lyricist turned composer-lyricist who created the score.

Ziegfeld Follies

135–137

Producer Florenz Ziegfeld (1867–1932) presented the first of his Follies in 1907, and continued offering them annually or almost annually through 1931.

---

135. In the 1918 *Ziegfeld Follies*, Lillian Lorraine sang "Any Old Time at All." Who are the 4 comedians surrounding her? This was also the first *Follies* appearance of what celebrated blonde dancer?

136. The *Ziegfeld Follies* of 1924 continued for over a year because of specially designated Spring and Summer Editions. Added to the cast of the Spring Edition were 2 favorite clowns, both seen in this sketch. Name the careless driver at the wheel and the comedienne playing the child in the broad-brimmed hat.

137. During the run of the 1924 *Follies*, the number "I'd Like to Corral a Gal" was added as a properly glamorous—if slightly incongruous—setting for the rope twirling of what folksy humorist?

Revues

138–141

Though seldom seen on Broadway anymore, the form of plotless musical known as the revue was a great favorite during the 20s and 30s.

———

138. What was Irving Berlin's theme song for all 4 editions of *The Music Box Revue*? The modestly garbed Adam and Eve shown here were played in a sketch in the 1924 edition by what 2 popular clowns?

139. The stellar threesome of a popular 1930 revue. Can you name them? Can you name it? What was the smoldering torch song introduced by the lady that became the hit of the show? Who wrote it? Name the revue offered the previous year in which these 3 also appeared.

140. In what revue did this debonair gentleman recall the vanished days of Palace vaudeville, and what was the song he sang and danced to? This was the third of a series of numerically progressive revues. Can you name the other 2?

141. A modern revue, based on a comic strip, had a lengthy run off-Broadway beginning in 1967. What was the show called and what is the name of the comic strip? Who is the actor on the right, seen as the title character, and what popular television series has he appeared in?

Shakespearean Sources

142–145

142. The 1938 musical *The Boys from Syracuse* was based on what 1594 comedy by Shakespeare? Can you identify the 3 actors in this scene? Who played the part of the twin brother of the actor on the right? Name the 2 top songs from the Rodgers and Hart score.

143. How to handle a woman, as demonstrated in *Kiss Me, Kate* (1948). What was the Shakespearean source of the play being produced in this backstage musical? Who were the 2 principal players? Who wrote the songs?

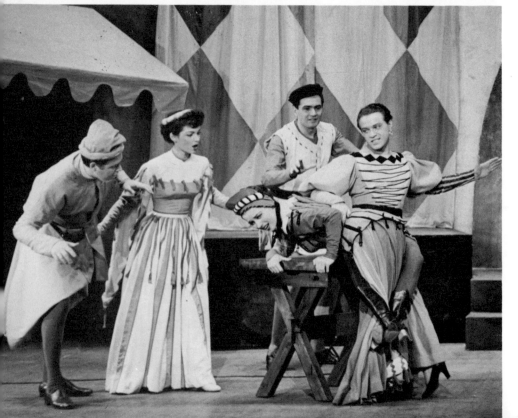

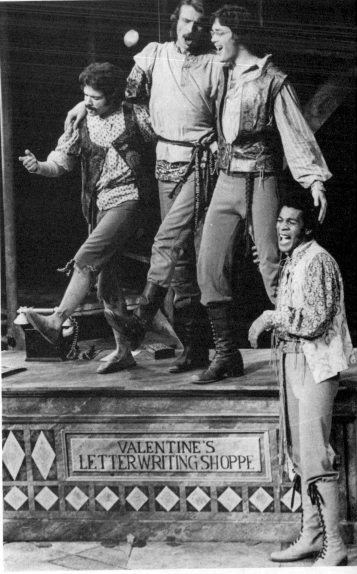

144. Shakespeare relocated to the streets of New York. What was the play that supplied the basic plot for *West Side Story*? Who are the principals shown here in this "balcony" scene, and what is the song they are singing?

145. What was this musical that, except for the loss of the definite article, had the same title as the Shakespearean play from which it was adapted? Can you identify the 2 actors on the right?

Classics into Musicals

146–151

146. Rodgers and Hammerstein's *Carousel* (1945) was adapted from a Hungarian fantasy written in 1909. What was the title, and who was the author? Name the 2 leading players in the musical. What was their love duet? For extra credit, who had the main parts when the original play was first presented on Broadway in 1921?

147. In this scene from *My Fair Lady* (1956), who are the 3 principals shown, what are they singing, and why are they singing? What was the Bernard Shaw play from which it was adapted? Can you name at least one other Shaw play that was transformed into a musical?

148. Who are the beaming actors pictured here and in what 1961 musical did they do the beaming? From whose melodies was the score adapted and mated to whose lyrics? From what Greek comedy by Aristophanes was the plot freely adapted?

149. In 1964, rubber-faced Bert Lahr starred in a musical version of what play written by what contemporary of Shakespeare? Who was Lahr's co-star, seen here in the flowered vest? Who were responsible for the score?

150. Miguel de Saavedra Cervantes'
novel *Don Quixote* was the source of the
musical *Man of La Mancha* (1965). In this
scene, the wounded Don is being comforted
by Aldonza and Sancho Panza, as the In-
keeper looks on. Who played these parts?
Who played Cervantes in the musical? What
was the musical's most popular song?

151. In what 1974 musical adaptation
of what classic French novel are these unin-
hibited young lovers cavorting? Do you
know who they are and what they are singing? Can you name the composer? Do you
recall who played these parts in the original
1956 production? What was the most unusual feature of the revised version?

Dance

152–157

---

152. In *On Your Toes* (1936), a "jazz ballet" served as both the climax of the show and as an important part of the plot. What was it called? Who was its classically trained Russian-born choreographer? Who was its composer? Can you identify the 3 principals shown here as The Hoofer, the Big Boss and the Strip Tease Girl?

153. Who were the 19th-century lithographers whose work was reflected both scenically and choreographically in this skating ballet from *Up in Central Park* (1945)? Who staged the dance and who supplied the score?

154. The hornpipe ballet from Rodgers and Hammerstein's *Carousel* (1945). Who was the choreographer? Do you recall the name of the dancer who played the hero's daughter and won plaudits for her dance on a beach later in the show?

155. Who was the choreographer of the sword dance that preceded the wedding in what highland fantasy? Can you identify the leading dancer? Who wrote the score for this musical? Name its most popular song.

156. A ballet and Broadway choreographer conceived the idea of updating the *Romeo and Juliet* tale so that it would be told primarily through frenetic dance movement, as in this scene at a high-school gym. Who was the choreographer and what was the musical?

157. Name the 1975 musical that concerned itself with Broadway's unsung dancing gypsies. What is the number being performed in this picture? Who is the man who put the show together?

Biographies

158–161

158. The only one-legged leading character in a musical was played by a dramatic actor in his only Broadway song-and-dance appearance. What was the part, who was the actor and what was the name of the musical? What was the most enduring Kurt Weill/Maxwell Anderson song in the score?

159. Alfred Drake tries vainly to calm the tempers of 2 jealous ladies in this musical based on the life of the early 19th-century actor named (a) Edwin Booth; (b) Edwin Forrest; (c) Edmund Kean; (d) William Macready; (e) none of the above. Who are the ladies and what was the name of the musical? Can you remember the name of the song being sung during this confrontation?

160. *Funny Girl* (1964) helped Barbra Streisand become an even bigger star than the comedienne she portrayed. Who was the comedienne, who was the man she loved and who played his part in the show? What was the song introduced in this scene in a private dining room, and who wrote it? For extra credit, in what off-Broadway revue did Miss Streisand make her professional debut?

161. A 1968 musical gave Broadway audiences the chance to see again the theatre's Yankee Doodle Boy as impersonated by a slim, agile dancing star. Who was impersonated and who did the impersonating? What was the show called? What was the song being rendered in this flag-waving number?

Pulitzer Prize Winners

162–165

Between 1918, when the award was first given, and 1976, when A Chorus Line *won, 5 musicals have been awarded the Pulitzer Prize for drama.*

162. In 1932, the first musical to win the prize was a satire on presidential elections. What was it called? In this scene, Victor Moore and William Gaxton, as candidates for vice president and president, are surrounded by advisers Sam Mann, Harold Moffet, Edward H. Robins, Dudley Clements and George E. Mack. What were the names of the characters played by Moore and Gaxton? Which one of the musical's writers—George Gershwin, Ira Gershwin, George S. Kaufman, Morrie Ryskind—was not cited by the Pulitzer committee and what was the reason?

163. What was this 1949 Pulitzer winner and what is the song being sung in this scene? Who are the people? Who wrote the score? What other musical by the same composer and lyricist was given a "special award" in 1943?

164. In this prizewinner of 1960, the hero, a rising political leader, is given a farewell party just before he goes overseas in World War I. What was the musical and who played the title role (far left)? Can you recall the song being sung, who wrote it, and the names of the other actors?

165. The 1962 prize went to a musical satire on big business, written by librettist Abe Burrows and composer-lyricist Frank Loesser. What was it called? Who are the players in this scene?

Musicals Adapted from Plays

166–171

166. The war between the Amazons and the Greeks made for a successful comedy in 1932 that became an even more successful musical 10 years later. What was the name of each? What is the song being sung by Ray Bolger and Bertha Belmore in the musical version and who wrote it? Who played the leading female role in the play, and who played it in the musical?

167. Carol Channing as she appeared in 1949 in *Gentlemen Prefer Blondes*. What was the name of the character she played, what song is she singing, and who wrote it? Who were the authors of the 1926 play from which the musical was adapted, and who was the original blonde in it? What was the name of the revised version of the musical which opened on Broadway in 1974, and who starred in it?

168. "The Musical with the Swimming Pool" was the way they billed this 1952 production about an adult summer camp. What was it called? Can you identify the 3 principals shown in this scene? Give the name of the Arthur Kober play on which the musical was based, and the names of its leading actors.

169. In 1925, Sidney Howard won the Pulitzer Prize for his play about an aging wine grower in California and his mail-order bride. What was it called, and who played the leads? In 1957, Frank Loesser won the Drama Critics Circle prize for his almost operatic version. What was it called, and who played the leads (pictured here)? What were the 2 most popular pieces in the score?

170. *Ah, Wilderness!* (1933), the only outright comedy written by Eugene O'Neill in his mature years, was a nostalgic look at smalltown America. Who had the parts in it that were later played in the musical version by the soft-shoeing Walter Pidgeon and Jackie Gleason? What was the name of the musical and the number Pidgeon and Gleason are performing?

171. What 1954 play about Noah and his ark was transformed into what 1970 musical? Who were involved in the writing of each? Who played Noah in each? Name another Odets play that was adapted as a musical.

From Screen to Musical Stage

172–179

172. What were the names of the films in the French trilogy—and who was their author—that was transformed into this 1954 Broadway musical? Who are the co-stars shown in this picture? Who created the score?

173. A Western film (with songs by Frank Loesser) became a 1959 Broadway musical with the same title (with a score by Harold Rome). What was it? In this scene from the stage production are Andy Griffith, Scott Brady and Dolores Gray. Who played their parts in the 1939 film?

From Screen to Musical Stage

continued

174. The story of a waif who joins a traveling carnival was filmed in 1953 with Leslie Caron as Lili and Kurt Kasznar as her sympathetic friend. What was the name of the 1961 stage musical and who now played the Caron and Kasznar roles?

175. The musical in which this scene takes place came after the story had already been filmed twice—the first time with Margaret Sullavan and James Stewart, the second with Judy Garland and Van Johnson. What were the titles of the films? What was the title of the stage musical? Who are these actors, and what song does the girl sing after the boy leaves?

176. An appealing fantasy about a real Santa Claus was first made as a 1947 movie called *The Miracle on 34th Street*. Who played Santa? Who played Santa in the 1963 stage musical called *Here's Love*? Name the leading lady and, if possible, anyone else shown in this scene. Who wrote the score?

177. The movie *The Apartment* (1960), starring Jack Lemmon and Shirley Mac-Laine, was a humorously sordid tale about getting ahead in a big corporation. What was the title of the 1968 musical version? Who had the leading roles? What Bert Bacharach/Hal David song is being performed here and why is it being performed?

178. The lusty, brawling hero of this musical had first been seen in a 1965 movie starring Anthony Quinn. What was the name of the show, what was the name of the character and who played him on the stage? Who was his co-star and what previous musical had they appeared in together?

179. A 1955 Swedish film about romantic entanglements at the turn of the century was turned into a highly praised stage musical of 1973. What was the film, what was the musical? Who directed the film? Who directed the musical and who wrote its score? Identify the actress whose hand is being kissed.

From Musical Stage to Screen

180–185

180. Obviously a romantic confrontation is brewing as stalwart Capt. James Stewart of the Texas Rangers (played by J. Harold Murray) frowns on the advances made by a Mexican general (Vincent Serrano) to his beloved Rio Rita (Ethelind Terry). When this 1927 musical was filmed in 1929, who played the romantic couple on the screen? What movie comedy team first appeared together in the stage musical and repeated their roles in this film? Who had the leading roles in the 1942 film remake?

181. Kern and Hammerstein's landmark musical *Show Boat*, which followed *Rio Rita* into the Ziegfeld Theatre the same year, was filmed 3 times: 1929, 1936 and 1951. Who played the characters of Cap'n Andy (Charles Winninger, the original Andy, is shown here), Magnolia, Gaylord Ravenal, Julie and Joe in all 3 movie versions?

182. In this nightclub scene (from what 1944 musical?), the actors are, from left to right, Allyn McLerie, Betty Comden, Adolph Green, Cris Alexander, Nancy Walker and John Battles. Who played their roles—except for Miss McLerie's—in the film version? Who wrote the libretto and lyrics for the original production and the screenplay and new lyrics for the movie? Who composed the original score?

183. What was this 1960 musical about a gold-hearted Parisian prostitute that came to Broadway from Paris via London? Who are the happy twosome with their arms outstretched, and who played their roles in the 1963 movie version? What was an unusual feature of the film?

184. Who are these 2 actors in a scene from what Alan Jay Lerner/Burton Lane musical about extrasensory perception? Who had their roles in the screen version?

185. What is the song being sung here by Joel Grey as the epicene German Master of Ceremonies in *Cabaret* (1966)? When the musical was filmed in 1972, his role was played by (a) Anthony Newley; (b) Ben Vereen; (c) Tommy Steele; (d) Bob Fosse; (e) none of the above. Who had the leading female role on stage and who had it on screen?

Revivals

186–191

---

186. When *Sweethearts,* the Victor Herbert/Robert B. Smith operetta, was revived in 1947, the book was drastically altered to build up the role played by the comedian at the right. Who is he? Can you also recognize the swooning lady? What was the name of the actress who starred in the original 1913 production? (She is shown in picture *3* in this book.)

187. What pioneering Rodgers and Hart musical of 1940 was revived a little over 11 years later and enjoyed even greater success? Identify the 2 principals shown in this photo. Who played their parts in the original production? What is the number being performed?

188. The 1971 revival of what 1925 Broadway musical brought what retired dancer back to the theatre after an absence of 41 years? Who is the actor she is dancing with in the final scene in the show? Name the composer and lyricist of the 2 biggest songs in the score. Name the leading actors in the original production.

189. Following the success of the above-mentioned revival, an even older musical was exhumed on Broadway. What was the show and who played the 2 leading female roles (shown here singing "Mother Angel Darling," an interpolated song by Charles Gaynor)? Who starred in the original production? Who wrote the original score?

190. The 1974 Broadway revival of *Gypsy* had been presented in London the previous year. Who played the role originated by Ethel Merman? What is the Jule Styne/Stephen Sondheim number she is performing here? Who had the leading part in the 1962 movie version?

191. A surprise hit came to Broadway late in 1975 when a 60-year-old musical was restored. What was the title? What Jerome Kern/Schuyler Greene song is being presented by this quartet of newlyweds?

Future Film Stars

192–199

192. Irving Berlin and the 8 lovelies known as the Eight Notes appeared together in a Broadway revue in 1921. Who is the eighth note on the far right of the second row? In 1930 she went to Hollywood, where she acted in over 30 films. What is the name of the revue which marked the actress' Broadway debut?

193. A musical-comedy leading man in 4 productions between 1927 and 1931, the actor on the right then left the stage to become one of Hollywood's most durable stars. What was his name when he appeared on Broadway and what was his name in films? He is seen here with Gladys Baxter and Hal Forde in *A Wonderful Night* (1929), one of the English-language adaptations of Johann Strauss's *Fledermaus*.

194. In this scene from a celebrated revue of 1930, singer Libby Holman pours her heart out to a *matelot* before he goes off to sea. What was the show, what was the song, and who played the French sailor?

195. The actor on the left had been seen briefly in the film *Footlight Parade* before returning to New York, where he appeared in Group Theatre productions. He is shown in one of them, an anti-war musical, in which he played a German soldier in a scene with Russell Collins. Who is he, what was the name of the musical, and who wrote it? Do you remember the actor's first major film role?

196. In his first leading part on Broadway, the dancing actor on the left scored so impressively that he was soon given an M-G-M contract. What's his name, and what was the musical? Who are the others in this scene? Name the popular song the actor introduced in this production.

197. *Best Foot Forward* (1941), a musical about a prom weekend at a prep school, took the girl on the left out of the chorus of *Panama Hattie* and gave the girl on the right her first part on Broadway. Who are they and what was the film in which they both made their screen debuts? Can you recall the name of the girl in the middle and the song that is being sung? Also, try naming at least 2 other popular songs from the Hugh Martin/Ralph Blane score.

Future Film Stars

continued

198. His Majesty King Somdetch P'hra Paarmendr Maha Mongkut of Siam. What musical did Yul Brynner appear in before Rodgers and Hammerstein's *The King and I* (1951)? What was his first major film role? For extra credit, in what film did he make his screen debut?

199. The dark-haired girl on the left was a member of the chorus of *The Pajama Game* (1954) when she temporarily replaced the principal dancer, Carol Haney, and was discovered by a Hollywood film producer. Who is she? Who is the man in the striped shirt and the girl just to his right? What song was introduced in this scene and who wrote it?

Future Television Stars

200–205

200. The performer playing the ossified college student in this scene from *Too Many Girls* (1939) also acted in the film version, married the star of that film and appeared with her in a long-running television situation comedy. Who is he and whom did he marry? Who are the others in this scene? Who wrote the show's score?

201. Who is the strutting male dancer and what was the name of his best-known television series? Can you name the musical in which he appears here with Colette Lyon, and the song they are performing?

202. Even before she had her own television program, this comedienne had made herself known through frequent guest appearances. In what musical—in which she made her stage debut—did she sing the Mary Rodgers/Marshall Barer song, "Shy"?

203. Angela Lansbury, in white, was the star of *Mame* (1966) and her friend, in black, later became the star of a highly popular television domestic-comedy series. Who is she, what is the Jerry Herman song being sung, and what is the name by which the actress is known to television viewers?

204. What imaginative 1966 production, with a score by Jerry Bock and Sheldon Harnick, featured these 3 stars in 3 separate one-act musicals? Who are they? What is the title of the one-act musical from which this scene is taken? Name the television series in which the man in the middle has had a leading role.

205. A 1970 musical about the rise of an international banking family gave this actor his first starring part. Later he became better known as television's Barney Miller. Name him and the musical.

Dramatic Actors in Musicals

206–213

206. Although the dark-haired actress on the right had made her Broadway debut in a musical revue over 22 years before, her appearance in this musical followed a film career exclusively devoted to nonmusical roles. Who is the actress and what is the musical? Who is the blonde actress with her, what is the song they are singing and why are they singing it? For extra credit, name

the above-mentioned revue.

207. In *The Music Man* (1957), Prof. Harold Hill, on the right, explains to his friend Marcellus why he prefers "The Sadder-but-Wiser Girl," which the two follow with a buoyant buck-and-wing. Though Hill was played by a 39-year-old actor who had never before been in a musical, his success in this production has made him a mainstay of the musical theatre ever since. Who is he and who is his chubby friend? Name at least 2 of the main songs from the Meredith Willson score.

208. This English-born actor is best remembered for his Shakespearean roles on Broadway, though he did appear in 2 musicals: *Ball at the Savoy* (London, 1933) and *Tenderloin* (New York, 1960). In which one is he seen in this photograph, and who wrote its songs?

209. Richard Burton's only appearance in a musical found him playing King Arthur to Julie Andrews' Guenevere. What was the musical, who wrote it, and what is the song with which the king is seen wooing his queen in the first scene? What was the musical's main romantic solo, introduced by what actor as Sir Lancelot?

210. Hollywood's Scarlett O'Hara and Blanche DuBois kicked up her heels for the only time in a musical about émigré white Russians living in Paris. Who is the actress (shown here dancing to "Wilkes-Barre, Pa." with Byron Mitchell) and what was the name of the 1963 musical? Who was her co-star?

211. *Coco* (1969) starred this highly charged actress in her only musical. Who was Coco? Who was responsible for the score? Who succeeded the actress during the run of the musical?

212. Who are the prancing twosome (singing "One of a Kind") in this scene from what 1970 musical about a theatre star who is upstaged by a scheming young actress? Who played the twosome in the 1950 movie and what was it called? Who played the schemer on screen and stage?

213. Though the actress in the bunny suit had appeared in 2 musicals early in the 40s, her subsequent roles have been in dramas or comedies—except for this appearance in a 1970 musical about the early life of the Marx Brothers. What is her name and the name of this show? Can you figure out which of the Marxes are being impersonated by, left to right, Irwin Pearl, Lewis J. Stadlen, Daniel Fortus and Alvin Kupperman?

Japanese Reprints

214–217

_____

214–217. Translations of Broadway musicals have been made in almost every country of the world, though nowhere have these shows been welcomed more enthusiastically than in Japan. Can you match the 4 photographs selected from among the following musicals that were produced by the Toho Company in Tokyo during the 60s?

    (a) *The Fantasticks*
    (b) *Fiddler on the Roof*
    (c) *How to Succeed in Business Without Really Trying*
    (d) *The King and I*
    (e) *Kiss Me, Kate*
    (f) *My Fair Lady*
    (g) *No Strings*
    (h) *Oklahoma!*
    (i) *The Sound of Music*
    (j) *South Pacific*

Is there anything unusual about the casting in **217**?

Long-Run Record Holders

218–224

---

218. The first production of the 30s to set the long-run record for a musical was a semiprofessional satirical revue sponsored by a labor union. What was the name of the show and what was the union? Who composed the score? Who are the characters being portrayed in this number called "Four Little Angels of Peace"?

219. *Hellzapoppin* (1938), a rough-and-tumble vaudeville-type revue, succeeded *Pins and Needles* as the long-run champ for musicals. Its 2 madcap stars were: (a) Weber and Fields; (b) Olsen and Johnson; (c) Abbott and Costello; (d) Smith and Dale; (e) none of the above. Behind them in this photo, the trio of impersonators known as the Radio Aces are doing takeoffs on what performers?

220. On July 12, 1961, this Lerner and Loewe musical bested the *Oklahoma!* record. Who is the actor in the middle, what part did he play and what song is he singing?

Long-Run Record Holders

continued

221. This landmark musical about farmers and cowmen held the long-run record from July 1946 to July 1961. What was its title during the pre-Broadway engagements? Who are the actors shown in the picture and what is the song they sing?

222. From September 1970 through July 20, 1971, *Hello, Dolly!* (which opened in 1964) was the queen of long-run musicals. Who are the actors seen in this nose-to-nose confrontation? What was the play by Thornton Wilder, based on another play by Thornton Wilder, that was the source of this musical?

223. At this writing, *Fiddler on the Roof* (1964) holds the long-run record not only for Broadway musicals but for Broadway nonmusicals as well. Besides Zero Mostel, pictured here leading the celebrants singing "To Life!," name at least 2 other actors who played Tevye on Broadway. Name at least 2 of the main songs in the Jerry Bock/Sheldon Harnick score. Who was the musical's director-choreographer?

224. Though it's an off-Broadway musical—and its theatre seats only 150—no list of long-running musicals would be complete without reference to this production that opened in May 1960 and is still around. Who played the original leads, pictured during the "Rape" sequence? Try to remember at least 2 of the chief songs in the Tom Jones/Harvey Schmidt score.

Answers

*Photos **A** through **F** appear on the covers.*

A. Ezio Pinza was succeeded as Emile deBecque by Ray Middleton, Roger Rico and George Britton; Mary Martin was succeeded as Nellie Forbush by Martha Wright and (temporarily) Cloris Leachman. DeBecque's aria "Some Enchanted Evening" followed soon after the brandy sniffing.

B. In *Guys and Dolls* (1950), adapted from Runyon's "The Idyll of Miss Sarah Brown," Robert Alda and Sam Levene were the concerned participants in the crap game. Also visible in the scene are Stubby Kaye (squatting) and B. S. Pully (holding the money). The song was "Luck Be a Lady."

C. The reason for the smiles: Jefferson's reunion with his wife, which presumably gave him the inspiration to write the Declaration of Independence. The actors are William Daniels (Adams), Howard Da Silva (Franklin), Betty Buckley (Martha) and Ken Howard (Jefferson). (Sherman Edwards was composer-lyricist of the score.)

D. *Company* (1970) starred Dean Jones (succeeded soon after the opening by Larry Kert), had a score by Stephen Sondheim and was directed and produced by Harold Prince. (Among those visible behind Jones are John Cunningham, Donna McKechnie, Susan Browning, Barbara Barrie and Elaine Stritch.)

E. Keith Andes played opposite Lucille Ball in *Wildcat* (1960), whose score included Miss Ball's self-introduction "Hey, Look Me Over" (by Cy Coleman and Carolyn Leigh).

F. In the score for *Hair* (1968) were such songs as "Good Morning Starshine," "Aquarius," "Where Do I Go?" and "Let the Sunshine In." The scene depicted shows "The Bed" number being performed by Steve Curry, supported by Steve Gamet (left) and Hiram Keller (right). The girl on the mattress is Shelley Plimpton. (The songs were written by Galt MacDermot, James Rado and Gerome Ragni.)

1. *Babes in Toyland* (1903) had a score by Victor Herbert and Glen MacDonough. The babes were played by William Norris and Mabel Barrison (at the foot of the wall).

2. Fritzi Scheff sang "Kiss Me Again" (lyric by Henry Blossom) as part of an extended musical sequence called "If I Were on the Stage." The scene in the photo shows a charity bazaar in the gardens of the Château de St. Mar. Others in the foreground near the heroine are Walter Percival (in uniform), William Pruette and Claude Gillingwater.

3. Christie MacDonald played Princess Bozena (score by Heinrich Reinhardt and Robert B. Smith).

4. *The Student Prince in Heidelberg* (1924) had a score by Sigmund Romberg and Dorothy Donnelly. The prince's big numbers are "Deep in My Heart, Dear," "Golden Days," "Drinking Song" and "Serenade."

5. In *The Vagabond King*, Dennis King led the singing of "Song of the Vagabonds," with lyric by Brian Hooker. (King also starred in 2 other Friml operettas, *Rose-Marie* and *The Three Musketeers.*)

6. (c). (For a scene from *A Wonderful Night*, see No. **193.**)

7. Fay Templeton and Victor Moore (in his first Broadway musical) were the sacrificing couple in the original production of Cohan's *Forty-Five Minutes from Broadway* (Cohan took over the male lead in a 1912 revival). Three out of the 5 songs in the score: "Mary's a Grand Old Name," "So Long, Mary" and "Forty-Five Minutes from Broadway."

8. The song was "You're a Grand Old Flag." Cohan's real father, Jerry Cohan, played his stage father.

9. *The Merry Malones.*

10. In 1937, Richard Rodgers and Lorenz Hart wrote the score and George S. Kaufman and Moss Hart the libretto for the FDR musical called *I'd Rather Be Right.* (*Hold Your Hats, Boys* was the show's working title.)

11. Vernon and Irene Castle were in *Watch Your Step*, the only Broadway musical in which they danced together. The contrapuntal song was "Play a Simple Melody."

12. "All Alone," sung into illuminated telephones by Grace Moore and Oscar Shaw on opposite sides of a darkened stage, was added to the last *Music Box Revue.*

13. William Gaxton, Vera Zorina, Victor Moore and Irene Bordoni were the chief attractions of *Louisiana Purchase.*

14. Sgt. Ezra Stone, Pvt. Julie Oshins and Cpl. Philip Truex cavorting through "The Army's Made a Man Out of Me."

15. William O'Neal (Buffalo Bill), Marty May (publicity man) and Ray Middleton (Frank Butler, the show's leading attraction) emphatically assert "There's No Business Like Show Business." Rodgers and Hammerstein produced *Annie Get Your Gun*, whose score was originally to have been written by Jerome Kern.

16. In *Mr. President*, the first couple of the land were played by Robert Ryan and Nanette Fabray.

17. Vivienne Segal and Carl Randall played the romantic leads in *Oh, Lady! Lady!!* The discarded song was "Bill." Other Princess Theatre musicals with music by Kern: *Nobody Home, Very Good Eddie* (see **191** for a scene from the 1975 revival), *Oh, Boy!* and—though it didn't actually play the Princess—*Leave It to Jane.*

18 & 19. In **19** are, left to right, Charles Winninger (Andy), Howard Marsh (Ravenal), Norma Terris (Magnolia), Edna May Oliver (Parthy Ann). Sammy White and Eva Puck are between Miss Terris and Miss Oliver. In **18** Helen Morgan is about to sing "Bill"—even though audiences knew that the man she really was pining for was named Steve.

20 & 21. The 2 scenes are from *Roberta*. **20** shows Bob Hope (in his first major role in a book musical) surrounded by Ray (then Raymond) Middleton, Tamara, Fay Templeton (in her last Broadway appearance) and George Murphy. Murphy later became U.S. Senator from California. In **21,** Hope tries to tear Middleton away from man-hungry Lyda Roberti as Sydney Greenstreet looks on disapprovingly.

22. Shown here in *Music in the Air* (1932) are Katherine Carrington, Al Shean and Walter Slezak. Shean had been the vaudeville partner of Ed Gallagher, with whom he performed a conversational ditty called "Mr. Gallagher and Mr. Shean."

23. The scene involves Robert Shackleton, Grace McDonald, Richard Quine (he later became a film director) and Eve Arden. The song was "All the Things You Are," lyric by Oscar Hammerstein.

24. The show was *Oh, Kay!* (1926), the star was Gertrude Lawrence and the 2 men in the center of the picture are Oscar Shaw and Victor Moore (also shown are Frank Gardner and Sascha Beaumont). The score included: "Maybe," "Someone to Watch Over Me," "Do Do Do," "Clap Yo' Hands."

25. The ingenue was 19-year-old Ruby Keeler (who would not show up on Broadway again until 41 years later) and the comedians were Eddie Jackson, Lou Clayton and Jimmy Durante. In Boston, Miss Keeler's new husband, Al Jolson, joined the show by singing "Liza" from the audience while his wife danced to it on the stage.

26. *Girl Crazy* gave a major career boost to Ginger Rogers, in her second Broadway appearance. The song was "But Not for Me," also sung by the comedian Willie Howard. For another young lady made famous by this show, see **72.**

27. Todd Duncan and Anne Brown played Porgy and Bess in 1935 and 1942. The 1953 Bess was Leontyne Price.

28. William Gaxton and Helen Broderick were in *Fifty Million Frenchmen.* Included in the score: "You Do Something to Me" and "You've Got That Thing."

29. The masquerading royal couple of *Jubilee* (1935) were Mary Boland and Melville Cooper. The number featured in this scene was "Me and Marie." The standards are "Begin the Beguine" and "Just One of Those Things."

30. The new ambassador to the Soviet Union in *Leave It to Me!* (1938) was Alexander P. Goodhue, played by Victor Moore. Sophie Tucker played his wife. (Their 5 daughters, to their left in the picture, are April, Mildred Chenaval, Ruth Daye, Audrey Palmer and Kay Picture.)

31. Charles Walters (later to direct such films as *Easter Parade* and *Lili)* and Betty Grable as seen in *DuBarry Was a Lady.*

32. Danny Kaye was starred for the first time in *Let's Face It!* (1941). Also in the scene are Houston Richards, Benny Baker, Mary Jane Walsh and Jack Williams. Kaye's show-stopper was "Melody in 4-F," written by Sylvia Fine (Mrs. Kaye) and Max Liebman.

33. Don Ameche and Hildegarde Neff starred in the 1955 stage musical, based on the 1939 film *Ninotchka,* which starred Greta Garbo and Melvyn Douglas. The 1955 screen version of *Silk Stockings* starred Fred Astaire and Cyd Charisse.

34. In *Dearest Enemy* the couple was played by Helen Ford and Charles Purcell. Their duets were "Here in My Arms," "Bye and Bye" and "Here's a Kiss."

35. Mark Twain's novel *A Connecticut Yankee in King Arthur's Court* emerged on the stage as *A Connecticut Yankee* (1927). William Gaxton played the Yankee, who wooed the fair Constance Carpenter with "My Heart Stood Still" and "Thou Swell."

36. That's future movie choreographer Busby Berkeley on the left in his only appearance in a Broadway musical. The song he introduced was

"You Took Advantage of Me." Also in this scene are Demaris Doré and the show's hero, Charles King.

37. *On Your Toes* brought together Luella Gear, Monty Woolley (later to achieve immortality as "The Man Who Came to Dinner") and Ray Bolger (also in the scene is dancer Demetrios Vilan). "There's a Small Hotel" was the leading romantic duet.

38. Mitzi Green (left), Alfred Drake (in dark suit) and Ray Heatherton (right) were among the babes in *Babes in Arms* (1937). Also in the scene are Rolly Pickert (polka-dot shirt), Aljan deLoville (pilot) and Wynn Murray. The songs were: "Where or When," "Babes in Arms," "I Wish I Were in Love Again," "Way Out West," "The Lady Is a Tramp," "Johnny One Note," "My Funny Valentine," "Imagine" and "All at Once."

39. Vera Zorina and Dennis King are singing "I Married an Angel." Vivienne Segal and Walter Slezak were also starred.

40. Celeste Holm played Ado Annie and Lee Dixon was Will. Her solo was "I Cain't Say No," and their duet was "All er Nothin'." *Oklahoma!* was adapted from Lynn Riggs's *Green Grow the Lilacs.*

41. The romantic leads in *Me and Juliet* were Bill Hayes (now the hero of television's No. 1 soap opera, *The Days of Our Lives)* and Isabel Bigley. Their duet was "I'm Your Girl." The music of "No Other Love" was the same as that of "Beneath the Southern Cross."

42. In *Flower Drum Song,* Miyoshi Umeki's reason for breaking her wedding contract is that she is an illegal alien. ("My back is wet," she explains.) The actor behind her to the right is Keye Luke (remembered as Charlie Chan's No. 1 son). Others in the scene are Ed Kenney, Juanita Hall and Eileen Nakamura.

43. Singing "No Way to Stop It" are Theodore Bikel, Marian Marlowe and Kurt Kasznar.

44. Vivienne Segal's first Broadway appearance was in the Sigmund Romberg/Herbert Reynolds operetta, in which she introduced "Auf Wiedersehn."

45. Louise Groody co-starred with Charles King in *Hit the Deck* (1927). Their duet was "Sometimes I'm Happy." Miss Groody had previously been seen as the admonished heroine of *No, No, Nanette.*

46. Starring in *Paris* (1928) was Irene Bordoni, who was accompanied on stage by Irving Aaronson and his Commanders.

47. Shown in the "Moanin' Low" scene from *The Little Show* is Libby Holman, whose dancing partner was Clifton Webb. (The song was written by Ralph Rainger and Howard Dietz.)

48. Nanette Fabray co-starred in *Love Life* (1948) with Ray Middleton.

49. Lotte Lenya sang her song about "Pirate Jenny" in the 1954 off-Broadway version of *The Threepenny Opera.* Kurt Weill (Lotte Lenya's husband) composed the score, whose English lyrics were written by Marc Blitzstein.

50. Appearing together in *Bells Are Ringing* (1956) were Judy Holliday and Sydney Chaplin. Miss Holliday's chief songs in the Jule Styne/Betty Comden/Adolph Green score were "Long Before I Knew You," "Just in Time" and "The Party's Over."

51. Elaine Stritch introduced Noël Coward's "The Little Ones' ABC" in *Sail Away.*

52. In *Sally* Marilyn Miller played a dishwashing drudge who dons a Russian costume and passes herself off as a famous ballerina at a party. Miss Miller was supported by comedians Leon Errol and Walter Catlett.

The standard from the Jerome Kern score is "Look for the Silver Lining" (lyric by B. G. DeSylva).

53. The left-to-right lineup of the principals in *Sunny:* Esther Howard, Joseph Cawthorn, Dorothy Francis, Clifton Webb, Miss Miller, Paul Frawley, Mary Hay and Jack Donahue (also in the cast were Borrah Minevitch, Pert Kelton and George Olsen's Orchestra). The leading songs were "Who?" and "Sunny."

54. Both George Gershwin (with lyricist Ira Gershwin) and Sigmund Romberg (with lyricist P. G. Wodehouse) shared the composing assignment for *Rosalie,* which also offered the dancing talents of Jack Donahue. The idea for the show emanated from the widely publicized 1926 visit of Queen Marie of Rumania to the United States.

55. *As Thousands Cheer* (1933) had the services of songwriter Irving Berlin and sketchwriter Moss Hart. In this sketch, chambermaid Marilyn Miller is seen with scrubwoman Ethel Waters, housekeeper Helen Broderick and waiter Clifton Webb. (Among the Berlin songs were "Easter Parade," "How's Chances" and "Not for All the Rice in China.")

56. Al Jolson as he appeared in *Sinbad.* During the show's tour, he introduced "Swanee" by George Gershwin and Irving Caesar. (Sigmund Romberg and Harold Atteridge were credited with most of the songs, but Jolson interpolated many of his specialties during the run.)

57. Both horse and musical were called *Big Boy.* Though later popularized by Eddie Cantor, "If You Knew Susie Like I Know Susie" (Joseph Meyer/B. G. DeSylva) was introduced in the show by Jolson.

58. Jobyna Howland appeared with Eddie Cantor in *Kid Boots* (1923). (Harry Tierney and Joseph McCarthy wrote the songs.)

59. The sport was horse racing and the show was called *Banjo Eyes* (also an Eddie Cantor nickname). Virginia Mayo, who was part of a "horse" act in the show, is at the far right. The musical, whose songs were by Vernon Duke, John Latouche and Harold Adamson, was adapted from the play *Three Men on a Horse.* In 1961 a second musical version was called *Let It Ride!*

60. Gertrude Lawrence and Harry Richman sang "Exactly Like You" (by Jimmy McHugh and Dorothy Fields) in the show. Jack Pearl was also in the cast.

61. The 3 musicals that were part of the program called *Tonight at 8:30* were "Shadow Play," "Red Peppers" and "Family Album." In the photograph Miss Lawrence and Mr. Coward are seen performing the title song from "We Were Dancing," which was otherwise without music.

62. *Lady in the Dark* was the only Broadway stage production in which Victor Mature appeared. Miss Lawrence's show-stopper was "The Saga of Jenny," which was written for her by Kurt Weill and Ira Gershwin.

63. The actress' final stage appearance was in *The King and I* (1951), by Rodgers and Hammerstein. Her first number in the play was "I Whistle a Happy Tune." Following Miss Lawrence's death in September 1952, her role was played by Constance Carpenter, who was then succeeded by Annamary Dickey and Patricia Morison.

64. Miss Lillie appeared with Clifton Webb in *She's My Baby,* whose score was written by Rodgers and Hart. Irene Dunne played the ingenue.

65. Noël Coward co-starred with Miss Lillie in *This Year of Grace.*

66. *Set to Music* (something of a revised version of Coward's London revue *Words and Music*) introduced Broadway audiences to Richard Haydn. Miss Lillie's numbers included "Mad About the Boy," "Weary of It All," "Three White Feathers," "I Went to a Marvellous Party" and "The Party's Over Now."

67. Edward Woodward and Tammy Grimes are in the scene with Beatrice Lillie. The musical was adapted by Hugh Martin and Timothy Grey from Noël Coward's *Blithe Spirit.*

68. Fred and Adele's first hit was *For Goodness Sake,* which was known as *Stop Flirting* when it was presented in London the following year. The dancers' trademark was called the "runaround" step (because that's what it was), and the team performed it in this musical to the music of "The Whichness of the Whatness" (by William Daly, Paul Lannin and Arthur Jackson).

69. In *Lady, Be Good!,* Fred and Adele introduced "Fascinating Rhythm," "Hang on to Me" and "Swiss Miss" (the "runaround" number), all by George and Ira Gershwin. "The Man I Love" was the casualty of the road.

70. It was with Grace McDonald that Fred danced "My One and Only" in *Funny Face.*

71. Fred's partner in *Gay Divorce* (1932) was Claire Luce, with whom he introduced Cole Porter's "Night and Day." The actor in the dressing gown is Erik Rhodes, who repeated his role of a professional corespondent in the show's film version, *The Gay Divorcee.* (The actor on the left in Roland Bottomley.)

72. She sang "I Got Rhythm" (shown here) and "Sam and Delilah" in *Girl Crazy,* by the Gershwins.

73. Ethel Merman sang "Blow, Gabriel, Blow" in *Anything Goes,* which had a score by Cole Porter. She also sang "You're the Top," "I Get a Kick Out of You" and "Anything Goes." Her co-stars were William Gaxton and Victor Moore.

74. In the show Jimmy played the captain of the Lark's Nest Prison polo team, who helps wealthy Ethel plan a coming-out party for released convicts. Also heading the cast was Bob Hope in his last stage appearance. Among Ethel's songs: "Down in the Depths," "It's De-Lovely" (with Hope), "Ridin' High" and "Red, Hot and Blue."

75. In *DuBarry Was a Lady,* Bert Lahr, as a nightclub washroom attendant in love with the star attraction (played by Ethel), accidentally slips himself a Mickey Finn and dreams he is Louis and Ethel is DuBarry. Mae West was the authors' original choice for the title role.

76. Joan Carroll was the name of the 8-year-old who appeared in *Panama Hattie* and recited a spoken patter to "Let's Be Buddies" because child-labor laws prevented her from singing. Betty Hutton (whose understudy was June Allyson) introduced "Fresh as a Daisy."

77. In 1950, Ethel Merman starred in Irving Berlin's *Call Me Madam,* whose story was sparked by the appointment of Perle Mesta to be ambassador to Liechtenstein. Paul Lukas was there for continental charm.

78. Ethel Merman, Sandra Church and Jack Klugman sang "Together" in *Gypsy,* which was based on a book by Gypsy Rose Lee. Also included in the Jule Styne/Stephen Sondheim score were "Some People," "You'll Never Get Away from Me," "Mr. Goldstone, I Love You," "Everything's Coming Up Roses," "Small World" and "Rose's Turn," all sung by Miss Merman.

79. Mary Martin sang "My Heart Belongs to Daddy" in *Leave It to Me!* (1938), which had a score by Cole Porter. The hoofer is Gene Kelly in his first Broadway appearance.

80. *One Touch of Venus* (1943). Shortly after her scene with John

Boles, Miss Martin sang "West Wind," by Kurt Weill and Ogden Nash.

81. Mary Martin toured for 9 months as Annie Oakley in *Annie Get Your Gun* while Ethel Merman played the part on Broadway.

82. Myron McCormick played Billis. Before and after this sequence the men expressed the way they felt in "There Is Nothin' Like a Dame." (For the same scene performed by a Japanese cast, see **215**.)

83. Miss Martin's songs were "The Sound of Music," "My Favorite Things" (with Patricia Neway), "Do-Re-Mi" (with children), "The Lonely Goatherd" (with children), "An Ordinary Couple" (with Theodore Bikel), "Edelweiss" (with Bikel and children). Bikel played the bridegroom in the wedding scene.

84. Mary Martin and Robert Preston played the married couple in *I Do! I Do!* (1966), by Tom Jones and Harvey Schmidt. The most memorable song: "My Cup Runneth Over." The most unusual feature of the production: Martin and Preston were the only ones in it.

85. Cole Porter's *Can-Can* (1953) starred Lilo, but it was Miss Verdon who got the rave notices. Her first Broadway appearance was in the revue *Alive and Kicking* in 1950.

86. In *Damn Yankees* (1955), Miss Verdon and Stephen Douglass sang "Two Lost Souls," written by Richard Adler and Jerry Ross. "Whatever Lola Wants (Lola Gets)" and "A Little Brains—a Little Talent" were also sung by Miss Verdon.

87. Gwen Verdon sang "If My Friends Could See Me Now" in this scene from *Sweet Charity* (1966). Cy Coleman and Dorothy Fields wrote the score (which also included "Big Spender," "There's Gotta Be Something Better than This" and "Where Am I Going?"). The musical was based on Federico Fellini's film *The Nights of Cabiria (Le notti di Cabiria)*.

88. The musical *Chicago* was adapted from the play of the same name. Miss Verdon's co-star was Chita Rivera, with whom she is seen singing "My Own Best Friend," by John Kander and Fred Ebb.

89. (d). Carol Channing, who originated the role in 1964, played it on Broadway for 19 months. She also toured in it during the 1965–66 and 1966–67 seasons.

90. (h). Mary Martin headed the first touring company—which also played the Far East and London—from April 1965 to May 1966.

91. (l). Ginger Rogers succeeded Miss Channing on Broadway and remained with the show 18 months. She also led a touring company from April 1967 to March 1968.

92. (f). Betty Grable was a touring Dolly from the end of 1965 to early 1967. She also starred on Broadway for 5 months in 1967.

93. (a). Eve Arden replaced Miss Channing on tour during the summer and early fall of 1966.

94. (k). Martha Raye followed Ginger Rogers on Broadway, heading the company for 4 months in 1967.

95. (g). Dorothy Lamour alternated the role with Ginger Rogers on tour between August and October 1967.

96. (b). Pearl Bailey starred in an all-black company that played on Broadway for 2 years and 2 months, beginning October 1967. She then toured for another 18 months.

The night spot was the Harmonia Gardens (it was there that Jerry Herman's title song was introduced). The show was produced by David Merrick and directed and choreographed by Gower Champion. (All 4 actresses whose pictures are not shown played the leading role on Broad-

way: Bibi Osterwald in November 1967; Thelma Carpenter alternating with Pearl Bailey; Phyllis Diller for 3 months beginning December 1969; and Ethel Merman for 9 months beginning March 1970.)

97. Bert Williams began his career with Walker, with whom he appeared until 1909 (also in the picture is Walker's wife, Aida Overton Walker). The song most associated with Williams was "Nobody" (by Williams and Alex Rogers), which he sang in almost every stage appearance.

98. *Shuffle Along* co-starred Flournoy Miller and Aubrey Lyles. The score included "I'm Just Wild About Harry" (this was a campaign song) and "Love Will Find the Way." (Florence Mills, later to become the toast of London in Lew Leslie's *Blackbirds*, and Josephine Baker, later to become the toast of Paris at the Folies Bergère, joined the cast of *Shuffle Along* during its run.)

99. Bill Robinson in *The Hot Mikado* (1939), which had to face the competition of the rival *Swing Mikado*, sponsored by the Chicago Federal Theatre.

100. Ethel Waters and Dooley Wilson (who later sang "As Time Goes By" in *Casablanca*) during a scene from *Cabin in the Sky*. Music for the show was written by Vernon Duke and the lyrics by John Latouche. The show-stopping song: "Taking a Chance on Love" (lyric by Ted Fetter and Latouche). (Arlen and Harburg wrote additional songs for the film version.)

101. George Bizet's *Carmen* became *Carmen Jones* thanks to the efforts of Oscar Hammerstein II. In the picture, Muriel Smith, in the title role, is singing "Dat's Love" (formerly the "Habanera").

102. Sammy Davis, Jr., his father and his uncle Will Mastin appeared together in *Mr. Wonderful*. In the score were the title song and "Too Close for Comfort."

103. Lena Horne starred in *Jamaica* with Ricardo Montalban. Among her songs were "Cocoanut Sweet," "Push de Button" and "Take It Slow, Joe." Miss Horne's Broadway debut was in the small role of "A Quadroon Girl" in the 1934 drama *Dance with Your Gods*.

104. In *No Strings* (1962), Diahann Carroll played Barbara and Richard Kiley played David. In this scene, she is singing "You Don't Tell Me," words and music by Richard Rodgers. Among the other songs: "The Sweetest Sounds," "Loads of Love," "Look No Further" and "No Strings."

105. Ben Vereen led the Players at the beginning of *Pippin* in singing "Magic to Do" (music and lyric by Stephen Schwartz). Bob Fosse was the show's director.

106. The Tinman (Tiger Haynes) receives his heart from the Wiz (Andre deShields) in *The Wiz* (score by Charlie Smalls). In 1903, *The Wizard of Oz*, starring Dave Montgomery as the Tin Woodman and Fred Stone as the Scarecrow, was adapted by L. Frank Baum from his popular children's fantasy *The Wonderful Wizard of Oz*.

107. Kate Smith sang "Red Hot Chicago," by B. G. DeSylva, Lew Brown and Ray Henderson, in *Flying High*. Bert Lahr is at the microphone.

108. Fanny Brice, Ted Healy and Phil Baker were co-starred in Billy Rose's *Crazy Quilt* (Miss Brice was then married to Rose). The trio sang "I Found a Million Dollar Baby (in a Five and Ten Cent Store)," by Mort Dixon, Billy Rose and Harry Warren. The previous version of the revue, also sponsored by Rose, was called *Sweet and Low*; Miss Brice, James

Barton and George Jessel headed the cast.

109. Helen Broderick played Queen Mary of England in this sketch dealing with the romantic activities of the Prince of Wales (played by Thomas Hamilton). At the left is George V (played by Leslie Adams).

110. Imogene Coca, though fully clad, performs a striptease.

111. *New Girl in Town* (1957), based on O'Neill's *Anna Christie*, co-starred Gwen Verdon and Thelma Ritter (in her only stage musical). Bob Merrill wrote the score.

112. Nancy Walker's effort to attract attention in *Do Re Mi* (1960) shocks not only Silvers but also mobsters George Givot, David Burns and George Mathews. The comedienne's show-stopper, "Adventure," was written by Jule Styne, Betty Comden and Adolph Green.

113. In *The Unsinkable Molly Brown* (1960), Tammy Grimes is introducing society leader Edith Meiser to her father Cameron Prud'homme, her husband Harve Presnell, and her titled friends Mony Dalmes and Mitchell Gregg. Meredith Willson wrote the score.

114. Kaye Ballard at the mercy of James Mitchell in *Carnival*. Their song was "Always Always You" (other numbers in the score were "Love Makes the World Go Round" and "Mira"). Miss Ballard's ballad in *The Golden Apple* was "Lazy Afternoon" (by Jerome Moross and John Latouche).

115. *Milk and Honey* marked the Broadway debut of Molly Picon, who was co-starred with Mimi Benzell and Robert Weede.

116. Strutting through the number are Tiger Haynes and Carol Burnett. Jule Styne, Betty Comden and Adolph Green supplied the songs for the show.

117. Fred and Dorothy Stone (and Fred's wife, Allene Crater) were all in *Stepping Stones*. "Raggedy Ann" was written by Jerome Kern and Anne Caldwell.

118. W. C. Fields appeared in *Poppy* (1923) as a carnival medicine man, Prof. Eustace McGargle. (The score was by Stephen Jones and Dorothy Donnelly.)

119. Bert Lahr (the boxer) and Victor Moore in *Hold Everything!* The big song: "You're the Cream in My Coffee."

120. Shown here are Jack Whiting, Robert Gleckler and Victor Moore. Whiting introduced "A Ship Without a Sail" in the musical.

121. Paul McCullough and Bobby Clark had the leading roles in *Strike Up the Band*, whose score by the Gershwin brothers included "Strike Up the Band!," "Soon" and "I've Got a Crush on You" (which had been introduced in *Treasure Girl* in 1928). "The Man I Love" was in the score of the original version of *Strike Up the Band*.

122. Starring in *Mexican Hayride* was Bobby Clark, and the lady bull-fighter was June Havoc.

123. In this scene from *The Cocoanuts* (1925), Groucho Marx, abetted by Chico, Zeppo and Harpo, is auctioning off lots during the Florida land boom (Groucho: "There's a viaduct." Chico: "Why-a duck, why-a no chicken?"). Margaret Dumont, Groucho's favorite foil, is also in the scene. Irving Berlin wrote the songs.

124. Joe Cook (right) and Dave Chasen (left). Kay Swift and Paul James wrote the score, which included the popular title piece.

125. Ed Wynn starred in *Simple Simon*, in which Alan Edwards and Doree Leslie played Prince Charming and Cinderella. Miss Etting's song was "Ten Cents a Dance."

126. Jack Haley appeared in *Higher and Higher*. Sharkey the seal stole the show.

127. Willie Howard introduced the character in the *George White Scandals of 1935* (whose songs were by Ray Henderson and Jack Yellen). During most of his career his brother Eugene was his partner.

128. Big Rosie played Jumbo in the 1935 musical of that name, and Jimmy Durante played circus press agent Claudius B. Bowers. In the Rodgers and Hart score were "Little Girl Blue," "My Romance" and "The Most Beautiful Girl in the World." The most unusual feature of the musical was that it was played on a circus ring rather than on a stage, with the interior of the Hippodrome Theatre reconstructed so that audiences sat in a banked, circus-like arena.

129. George S. Kaufman wrote the sketch about a proud father's horrified discovery that his daughter is a virgin. Shown here are Helen Broderick, Adele Astaire, Frank Morgan and a bewigged Fred Astaire. Together the Astaires introduced the following Arthur Schwartz/Howard Dietz songs: "Sweet Music," "I Love Louisa," "Hoops" and "White Heat."

130. Fanny Brice appeared as Baby Snooks in this sketch with Bob Hope. The titular producer of this edition was Billie Burke Ziegfeld, the producer's widow, but it was actually sponsored by the Shubert brothers.

131. *Lady in the Dark* (1941) gave Danny Kaye his first major role. In the scene depicted he is shown with Gertrude Lawrence and, on the left, Margaret Dale. Kaye's song specialty was called "Tschaikowsky." His first Broadway appearance was in *The Straw Hat Revue* (1939).

132. Phil Silvers is being apprehended by Mark Dawson, Jack McCauley and Nanette Fabray. The songs were written by Jule Styne and Sammy Cahn.

133. Sid Caesar and Virginia Martin in a scene from *Little Me* (1962). The show was based on the book by Patrick Dennis, whose *Auntie Mame* had previously been made into the musical called *Mame*. (The songs in *Little Me* were by Cy Coleman and Carolyn Leigh.)

134. That's John Carradine on the left and Zero Mostel on the right in a scene from *A Funny Thing Happened on the Way to the Forum* (1962). Words and music were by Stephen Sondheim.

135. Surrounding Miss Lorraine: W. C. Fields, Will Rogers (in formal dress for the first time), Eddie Cantor (his first *Follies* minus blackface) and Harry Kelly. Marilyn Miller made her *Follies* debut in 1918.

136. W. C. Fields and Ray Dooley.

137. Will Rogers.

138. "Say It with Music" was the theme song. Bobby Clark and Fanny Brice played Adam and Eve in a sketch by Bert Kalmar and Harry Ruby.

139. Clifton Webb, Libby Holman and Fred Allen in *Three's a Crowd*. The song was "Body and Soul," by Johnny Green, Edward Heyman and Robert Sour. The trio previously appeared together in *The Little Show*.

140. Ray Bolger sang and danced "The Old Soft Shoe" (by Morgan "Buddy" Lewis and Nancy Hamilton) in *Three to Make Ready* (1946). The other 2 revues were *One for the Money* (1939) and *Two for the Show* (1940).

141. Clark Gesner's *You're a Good Man, Charlie Brown* was based on *Peanuts*. Gary Burghoff, who has become familiar to television viewers as Radar in *M.A.S.H.*, played Charlie Brown. (Others in the picture are Karen Johnson as Patty, Bob Balaban as Linus, Skip Hinnant as Schroeder, Reva Rose as Lucy and Bill Hinnant as Snoopy.)

142. *The Boys from Syracuse* was based on *The Comedy of Errors*. In the scene are Betty Bruce, Eddie Albert and Jimmy Savo. Savo's twin was played by Teddy Hart (brother of lyricist Lorenz Hart). The score included "Falling in Love with Love" and "This Can't Be Love."

143. *The Taming of the Shrew* (1594). Alfred Drake and Patricia Morison were the tamer and the tamee. Cole Porter wrote the songs (which included "So in Love," "Wunderbar" and "Always True to You in My Fashion").

144. Shakespeare's *Romeo and Juliet* (1597) was adapted for the 1957 musical. In this scene, Larry Kert and Carol Lawrence sing "Tonight" (by Leonard Bernstein and Stephen Sondheim).

145. *Two Gentlemen of Verona* (1971) stemmed from *The Two Gentlemen of Verona* (1595). In the picture are, left to right, José Perez, John Bottoms, Raul Julia and Clifton Davis. (The score was by Galt MacDermot and John Guare.)

146. *Carousel* was adapted from Ferenc Molnar's *Liliom*. Jan Clayton and John Raitt, who played the leads in the musical, sang "If I Loved You." Eve LeGallienne and Joseph Schildkraut appeared in *Liliom* in 1921.

147. Robert Coote, Julie Andrews and Rex Harrison perform "The Rain in Spain," in a joyous celebration of Miss Andrews' ability to speak proper English. The Alan Jay Lerner/Frederick Loewe musical was based on *Pygmalion*. Shaw's *Arms and the Man* became *The Chocolate Soldier* (music by Oscar Straus), and his *Caesar and Cleopatra* became *Her First Roman* (music and lyrics by Ervin Drake).

148. Janice Rule and Cyril Ritchard in *The Happiest Girl in the World*. The musical's music was based on Offenbach and its lyrics were by E. Y. Harburg. The basis for the plot was *Lysistrata* (411 B.C.).

149. *Foxy* (1964) was a musical version of Ben Jonson's *Volpone* (or *The Fox*). Larry Blyden and the thirsty Robert H. Harris were also in the musical, whose score was written by Robert Emmett Dolan and Johnny Mercer.

150. Don Quixote was played by Richard Kiley (who also played Cervantes), Aldonza by Joan Diener, Sancho Panza by Irving Jacobson and the Innkeeper by Ray Middleton. "The Impossible Dream," by Mitch Leigh and Joe Darion, was the musical's most popular song.

151. *Candide,* adapted from Voltaire's novel, featured Mark Baker in the title role and Maureen Brennan as his beloved Cunegonde, here singing "Oh Happy We," by Leonard Bernstein and Richard Wilbur. In 1956, the parts were played by Robert Rounseville and Barbara Cook. The most unusual aspect of the 1974 production was that director Harold Prince had the seating area of the Broadway Theatre rearranged so that the audience became virtually part of the performance.

152. "Slaughter on Tenth Avenue" was choreographed by George Balanchine and composed by Richard Rodgers. The scene involves Ray Bolger, George Church and Tamara Geva.

153. The Currier and Ives ballet had Helen Tamiris as choreographer. Sigmund Romberg was the show's composer and Dorothy Fields its lyricist.

154. Agnes de Mille choreographed the dances. Bambi Linn was the featured dancer in the beach ballet.

155. In *Brigadoon* (1947), the choreography was by Agnes de Mille, and the chief dancer was James Mitchell. "Almost Like Being in Love" was the hit of the Frederick Loewe/Alan Jay Lerner score.

156. George Balanchine and *West Side Story* (score by Leonard Bernstein and Stephen Sondheim).

157. The number being performed in *A Chorus Line* is "One" (by Marvin Hamlisch and Edward Kleban). Michael Bennett was the show's progenitor, director and choreographer. (Shown in the photograph, left to right: Sammy Williams, Pamela Blair, Michel Stuart, Nancy Lane, Cameron Mason, Renee Baughman, Ron Kuhlman, Patricia Garland, Thomas J. Walsh, Carole—now Kelly—Bishop, Don Percassi.)

158. Walter Huston played New Amsterdam Governor Pieter Stuyvesant in *Knickerbocker Holiday* (1938), in which he introduced "September Song."

159. Alfred Drake starred as Edmund Kean in *Kean* (1961). With Joan Weldon and Lee Venora he introduced "Civilized People" in this scene. (The score was written by Robert Wright and George Forrest.)

160. Barbra Streisand played Fanny Brice and Sydney Chaplin played Nick Arnstein in *Funny Girl*. The song presented in this scene was "You Are Woman," by Jule Styne and Bob Merrill. Miss Streisand's first professional appearance in New York was in *Another Evening with Harry Stoones* (1961).

161. Shown here singing "You're a Grand Old Flag," Joel Grey made like George M. Cohan in *George M!*

162. In *Of Thee I Sing* (1931), Moore played Alexander Throttlebottom and Gaxton was John P. Wintergreen. Composer George Gershwin was denied participation in the award on the technality, since repealed, that the prize could be awarded only for dramatic literature.

163. Rodgers and Hammerstein and Joshua Logan won the Pulitzer for *South Pacific* (R and H's "special award" had been for *Oklahoma!*). In this scene, Juanita Hall sings "Happy Talk," Betta St. John makes the appropriate hand gestures and William Tabbert is completely smitten.

164. Singing "Till Tomorrow" in *Fiorello!* (1959) are Tom Bosley (as Fiorello LaGuardia), Patricia Wilson, Nathaniel Frey and Ellen Hanley. The score was written by Jerry Bock and Sheldon Harnick, who shared the prize with librettists George Abbott and Jerome Weidman.

165. Seen in a slightly embarrassing position in *How to Succeed in Business Without Really Trying* (1961) are Bonnie Scott, Robert Morse and, in his first Broadway appearance in 30 years, Rudy Vallée.

166. *The Warrior's Husband* was musicalized as *By Jupiter*. In the picture, Bolger and Belmore (she had appeared in the 1932 play but in a different part) are singing Rodgers and Hart's "Life with Father." Katharine Hepburn had the leading female role in the play, which was taken by Constance Moore in the musical.

167. Miss Channing played Lorelei Lee and sang the Jule Styne/Leo Robin "Diamonds Are a Girl's Best Friend" in *Gentlemen Prefer Blondes*. Anita Loos and John Emerson wrote the original play, which had the same title, with June Walker playing Lorelei. Miss Channing also appeared in the revised musical version called *Lorelei*.

168. *Wish You Were Here* (score by Harold Rome) was the musical version of *Having Wonderful Time*. In the picture are Jack Cassidy, Patricia Marand and Sheila Bond. The romantic leads in the Kober play were Katherine Locke and Jules (later John) Garfield.

169. *They Knew What They Wanted* was the Howard play in which Richard Bennett and Pauline Lord had the leading roles. *The Most Happy Fella* was the Loesser musical with Robert Weede and Jo Sullivan in the leads. "Standing on the Corner" and "Big D" were the most popular pieces.

170. George M. Cohan and Gene Lockhart had the parts in the O'Neill play that Pidgeon and Gleason had in the musical version, *Take Me Along* (1959). In this scene, they are singing the title number. (Bob Merrill wrote the score.)

171. *The Flowering Peach,* by Clifford Odets, was transformed into *Two by Two* by librettist Peter Stone, composer Richard Rodgers and lyricist Martin Charnin. Menasha Skulnik was the first Noah, Danny Kaye the second. (In the photo he is shown with Harry Goz and Joan Copeland.) Odets' *Golden Boy* was also adapted as a musical, which retained the original title.

172. Marcel Pagnol's trilogy, *Marius* (1931), *Fanny* (1932) and *César* (1934) became *Fanny* on Broadway. Ezio Pinza and Walter Slezak were co-starred, and Harold Rome was responsible for the score. (The first English-language film adaptation was made in 1938 as *Port of Seven Seas*, with Wallace Beery and Frank Morgan; the stage musical was filmed in 1960 with Charles Boyer and Maurice Chevalier—but the Rome music was used only in the background.)

173. In the 1939 film *Destry Rides Again,* the parts were played by James Stewart, Brian Donlevy and Marlene Dietrich. The story was also filmed in 1932 and 1954.

174. *Carnival* was the stage musical adapted from *Lili,* with Anna Maria Alberghetti and Pierre Olaf in the Caron and Kasznar roles.

175. The films were *The Shop Around the Corner* (1940) and *In the Good Old Summertime* (1949). The stage musical was called *She Loves Me* (1963). The actors seated on the bed are Daniel Massey and Barbara Cook, who, after the boy leaves, will sing "Ice Cream" (by Jerry Bock and Sheldon Harnick).

176. Edmund Gwenn was the movie Santa; Laurence Naismith was the stage Santa. The vocal quintet harmonizing Meredith Willson's "My State" are Paul Reed, Janis Paige, Cliff Hall, Fred Gwynne and Arthur Rubin.

177. *Promises, Promises* was the name of the musical version. In the scene, Jerry Orbach (in hat) and A. Larry Haines try to cheer up Jill O'Hara (who has just tried to commit suicide) by singing and clowning through "A Young Pretty Girl Like You."

178. Zorbá was both the name of the character Herschel Bernardi played and the title of the 1968 stage musical (score by John Kander and Fred Ebb). Maria Karnilova co-starred with Bernardi—as she had previously done in *Fiddler on the Roof* (Bernardi replaced Zero Mostel).

179. Ingmar Bergman's *Smiles of a Summer Night* was the film; Harold Prince's and Stephen Sondheim's *A Little Night Music* was the musical. Glynis Johns (in her first musical role) is the actress having her hand kissed (by Laurence Guittard). Others in the scene: Patricia Elliott, Judy Kahan and Sherry Mathis.

180. The romantic couple in the first movie version of *Rio Rita* was played by Bebe Daniels and John Boles. Bert Wheeler and Robert Woolsey appeared in both stage and screen productions. The later film version starred Bud Abbott and Lou Costello, Kathryn Grayson and John Carroll. (The score was written by Harry Tierney and Joseph McCarthy.)

181. Cap'n Andy: Otis Harlan (1929), Charles Winninger (1936), Joe E. Brown (1951). Magnolia: Laura LaPlante (1929), Irene Dunne (1936), Kathryn Grayson (1951). Ravenal: Joseph Schildkraut (1929), Allan Jones (1936), Howard Keel (1951). Julie: Alma Rubens (1929), Helen Morgan (1936), Ava Gardner (1951). Joe: Stepin Fetchit (1929), Paul Robeson (1936), William Warfield (1951).

182. When *On the Town* was filmed in 1949, the roles were played by Ann Miller, Jules Munshin, Frank Sinatra, Betty Garrett and Gene Kelly. Betty Comden and Adolph Green wrote story and lyrics for both. Leonard Bernstein was the original composer (the film retained only about half his score and substituted new songs by Roger Edens with Comden and Green).

183. In *Irma la Douce,* the leads were played by Keith Michel and Elizabeth Seal on stage, and by Jack Lemmon and Shirley MacLaine on screen. The movie failed to use any of the original score by Marguerite Monnot, David Heneker, Julian More and Monty Norman. (Among the actors in the scene from the play are Fred Gwynne, George S. Irving and Clive Revill.)

184. John Cullum and Barbara Harris were in *On a Clear Day You Can See Forever* (1965), and Yves Montand and Barbra Streisand played their roles in the movie (1970).

185. Joel Grey, who appeared in both the stage and screen productions of *Cabaret,* is shown here singing "Willkommen" (by John Kander and Fred Ebb). Liza Minnelli had the Jill Haworth role in the movie.

186. Bobby Clark starred in the revived and revised *Sweethearts,* in which he is shown in a scene with Robert Shackleton and June Knight. Christie MacDonald played the heroine in the original production. (In 1913 the show ran 136 performances, in 1947 it ran 288.)

187. The principals in the revival of *Pal Joey* were Harold Lang and Vivienne Segal, here seen in the "Pal Joey" number that closed the first act. Miss Segal also appeared in the original opposite Gene Kelly. (In 1940 the show ran 374 performances; in 1952 it ran 542.)

188. Ruby Keeler returned to Broadway in *No, No, Nanette,* in which Bobby Van also had a prominent part. In the Vincent Youmans score: "Tea for Two" and "I Want to Be Happy," with lyrics by Irving Caesar. In the original New York production, Louise Groody and Charles Winninger had the featured roles (not the ones played by Miss Keeler and Mr. Van). (In 1925 the show ran 321 performances; in 1971 it ran 861.)

189. *Irene,* which dated from 1919, was revived in 1973 with Debbie Reynolds as Irene and Patsy Kelly as her mother. Edith Day starred in the original, which had a score by Harry Tierney and Joseph McCarthy (including the title song and "Alice Blue Gown"). (In 1919 the show ran 670 performances: in 1973 it ran 605.)

190. Angela Lansbury performing the dazzling "Rose's Turn" in *Gypsy.* Rosalind Russell played the role in the movie. (In 1959 the show ran 702 performances; in 1974 it ran 120.)

191. In *Very Good Eddie,* newlyweds Nicholas Wyman, Virginia Seidel, Charles Repole and Spring Fairbank sang "Isn't It Great to Be Married?" (The quartet in 1915 consisted of John Willard, Alice Dovey, Ernest Truex and Helen Raymond.)

192. Miriam Hopkins in the *Music Box Revue of 1921.*

193. Archie Leach became Cary Grant. (For a scene from another English-language version of *Die Fledermaus,* see **6**.).

194. The show was *Three's a Crowd,* the song was "Something to Remember You By" (by Arthur Schwartz and Howard Dietz) and the *matelot* was Fred MacMurray, whose main film career began in 1934.

195. John (then Jules) Garfield was in *Johnny Johnson* (1936). The score was written by Kurt Weill and Paul Green. His first major film role was in *Four Daughters* (1938).

196. Shown in a scene from Rodgers and Hart's *Pal Joey* (1940) are Gene Kelly, June Havoc and Jack Durant. Kelly introduced "I Could Write a Book."

197. June Allyson and Nancy Walker, who made their screen bows in the 1943 film version of *Best Foot Forward*. Victoria Schools is the third girl in the photo; their song was "The Three B's" ("The barrelhouse, the boogie-woogie and the blues"). Other songs in the score: "Ev'rytime," "Shady Lady Bird," "Buckle Down Winsocki" and "Just a Little Joint with a Jukebox."

198. Yul Brynner acted with Mary Martin in *Lute Song* (1946). His first screen appearance was in *Port of New York* (1949), and his first major film role was in the 1956 screen version of *The King and I*.

199. Seen behind stars John Raitt and Janis Paige is Shirley MacLaine during the "Once-a-Year Day" number. "Hey, There," "Steam Heat" and "Hernando's Hideaway" were also in the Richard Adler/Jerry Ross score.

200. Desi Arnaz, who later married Lucille Ball, is seen in *Too Many Girls* with fellow college students Eddie Bracken, Hal LeRoy and Marcy Westcott. The score was written by Richard Rodgers and Lorenz Hart ("I Didn't Know What Time It Was," "Love Never Went to College").

201. Long before acting in television's *Beverly Hillbillies*, Buddy Ebsen appeared in Broadway revues and—pictured here—a 1946 revival of the Kern/Hammerstein *Show Boat*. Joe Howard's "Goodbye, My Lady Love" is the song.

202. Carol Burnett first stage appearance was as the comic heroine of *Once Upon a Mattress* (1959).

203. Beatrice Arthur, television's Maude, was considerably slimmer when she sang "Bosom Buddies" with Angela Lansbury in *Mame*.

204. Larry Blyden, Alan Alda and Barbara Harris as they appeared in "The Lady or the Tiger" (the other two musicals that went under the collective title of *The Apple Tree* were "Adam and Eve" and "Passionella"). Alda has played the lead in television's *M.A.S.H.*

205. Hal Linden in *The Rothschilds* (score by Jerry Bock and Sheldon Harnick).

206. In *Wonderful Town* (1953), Rosalind Russell and Edie (then Edith) Adams revealed their homesickness through the song "Ohio" (by Leonard Bernstein, Betty Comden and Adolph Green). Miss Russell's Broadway debut had been in the second editon of the 1930 *Garrick Gaieties*.

207. Robert Preston and Iggy Wolfington. Other songs from *The Music Man*: "Seventy-Six Trombones," "Till There Was You," "Goodnight, My Someone."

208. Maurice Evans as he appeared in *Tenderloin*, which had music and lyrics by Jerry Bock and Sheldon Harnick.

209. Richard Burton wooed Julie Andrews with the title song from *Camelot* (1960), written by Alan Jay Lerner and Frederick Loewe. Robert Goulet sang "If Ever I Would Leave You."

210. *Tovarich* co-starred Vivien Leigh and Jean Pierre Aumont. (The score was written by Lee Pockriss and Anne Croswell.)

211. Katharine Hepburn's only musical was about the life of the French couturière Coco Chanel. Alan Jay Lerner and Andre Previn wrote it. Danielle Darrieux succeeded Miss Hepburn during the run.

212. Len Cariou and Lauren Bacall in *Applause* had the parts originated by Gary Merrill and Bette Davis in the film *All About Eve*. Anne Baxter, who succeeded Miss Bacall on Broadway, played the young actress on screen; Penny Fuller played it on stage. (Charles Strouse and Lee Adams wrote the songs.)

213. Shelley Winters, whose early musicals were *Rosalinda* and *Oklahoma!*, starred in *Minnie's Boys*. Chico was played by Pearl, Groucho by Stadlen, Harpo by Fortus and Zeppo by Kupperman. (The score was written by Larry Grossman and Hal Hackaday.)

214. (c). The "Grand Old Ivy" number, with Kyu Sakamoto as the ambitious J. Pierpont Finch and Keaton Masuda (he was named after Buster) as J. B. Biggley (1963).

215. (j). Nurse Nellie Forbush (Fubuki Koshiji) admiring the laundry work of Luther Billis (Kiyoshi Atsumi), much to the derision of the sailors and Seabees (1966). (See **82** for the same scene as performed by the original New York company.)

216. (b). Tevye and Golde sing "Do You Love Me?" Hisaya Morishige and Fubuki Koshiji played the parts (1967).

217. (h). The rousing "Oklahoma" finale. Note that the Takarazuka Revue Company—led by Noboru Kozuki as Curly and Jun Hatsukaze as Laurey—consists entirely of females (1967).

218. The International Ladies Garment Workers Union (ILGWU) sponsored *Pins and Needles* (1937). Harold Rome composed the score (including "Sunday in the Park," "It's Better with a Union Man," "Sing Me a Song with Social Significance"). The "Four Little Angels" are a Japanese General (Murray Modick), Hitler (Paul Seymour), Mussolini (Al Eben) and Anthony Eden (Hy Gardner). (During the run of the show, Eden was dropped in favor of Chamberlain, and later a fifth "Angel," Stalin, was added.) The show ran 1,108 performances.

219. Ole Olsen and Chic Johnson were the perpetrators of *Hellzapoppin*. Being impersonated are Edward G. Robinson (by Sidney Chatton), George Arliss (by Jimmy Hollywood) and Ed Wynn (by Eddie Bartel). (Sammy Fain and Charles Tobias wrote most of the songs.) The show ran 1,404 performances.

220. Stanley Holloway, accompanied by Gordon Dilworth and Rod McLennon, sings "With a Little Bit of Luck" in *My Fair Lady* (1956). The show ran 2,717 performances.

221. Rodgers and Hammerstein's *Oklahoma!* (1943) started life under the title *Away We Go!* Howard Da Silva and Alfred Drake are singing "Pore Jud." The show ran 2,212 performances.

222. David Burns and Ginger Rogers (Carol Channing's successor in the starring role) as Horace Vandergelder and Dolly Gallagher Levi. Wilder's *The Matchmaker*, based on Wilder's *The Merchant of Yonkers*, was the source of the musical. The show ran 2,844 performances.

223. Other Tevyes besides Mostel: Luther Adler, Herschel Bernardi, Harry Goz, Jerry Jarrett, Paul Lipson, Jan Peerce. The score included "Sunrise, Sunset," "If I Were a Rich Man" and "Miracle of Miracles." The director-choreographer was Jerome Robbins. The show ran 3,242 performances.

224. Jerry Orbach, Rita Gardner and Kenneth Nelson were in the original company of *The Fantasticks*. "Try to Remember," "Soon It's Gonna Rain," and "Much More" are among the songs. The show keeps running.

Index of Performers

Only the performers in the photographs are indexed. The numbers are those of the photographs
*(**A** through **F** appear on the covers).*

Index of Shows

Only the shows in the photographs are indexed. The numbers are those of the photographs
(**A** through **F** appear on the covers).